THE EPISTLES
OF JOHN

By Lehman Strauss

The Epistles of John
Devotional Studies in
    Philippians
Devotional Studies in
    Galatians and Ephesians
James, Your Brother
Certainties for Today
The Third Person
The Second Person
The Eleven Commandments
We Live Forever
An Examination of the Teaching
    of Modernism
An Examination of the Doctrine
    of Jehovah's Witnesses

THE EPISTLES OF
JOHN

BY

LEHMAN STRAUSS

LOIZEAUX BROTHERS
New York

FIRST EDITION, JULY 1962

Library of Congress Catalog Card Number: 62-17542

PRINTED IN THE UNITED STATES OF AMERICA

PREFATORY NOTE

This little volume could never have been written were it not for the many others who made contributions to my life and labors. I am indebted to those who have written on this Epistle and from whose writings I have drawn, and to the Misses Elsa Dearborn and Lila Sargeant, for their tireless efforts in typing the manuscript and preparing the indices.

LEHMAN STRAUSS

Highland Park, Michigan

TABLE OF CONTENTS

THE FIRST EPISTLE OF JOHN

Part One

THE PENMAN OF THE EPISTLE

I. THE PENMAN OF THE EPISTLE

Some Passages common to the First Epistle and the Gospel

First Epistle of John	Gospel according to John
1:1; 5:7	1:1,14
1:4	15:11
1:8; 3:5	9:41; 15:22,24
2:1	14:16,26; 15:26; 16:7
2:11	12:35
3.1,13	15:18,19; 17:14,25
3:8	8:44
3:16	15:13
5:12	3:36

While this Epistle bears the name of John, it has neither address nor signature, and is therefore anonymous. Most scholars agree, however, that the apostle who wrote the fourth Gospel record is likewise the writer of this Epistle. There seems to be no good reason for rejecting the tradition that five documents in the New Testament were penned by the Apostle John, the son of Zebedee.

One could wish that this Epistle had included the name of the man whom God used to pen its words. Elsewhere we read: "Paul . . . to all that be in Rome" (Romans 1:1,7), and so with all of Paul's Epistles; "James . . . to the twelve tribes" (James 1:1); "Peter . . . to the strangers scattered . . ." (1 Peter 1:1); "Jude . . . to them that are sanctified by God the Father . . ." (Jude 1). But here there is no "John" in the Epistle itself; it is both unaddressed and unsigned.

The common authorship of the Gospel, the Epistle, and the Revelation is implied in the use of the significant term *"Logos."* It is applied to our Lord only in these three books. This is a strong argument for all three having come from the same pen (John 1:1,14; 1 John 1:1; 5:7; Revelation 1:2; 19:13).

Another expression common to John is in chapter 1:8, in the words "have no sin." I refer to the use of the verb *have* in connection with sin. Elsewhere the Scriptures speak of *committing* sin, but not to *have* it. (See John 9:41; 15:22,24; 19:11). What is meant is that the sin principle is inherent in us. We possess it. It is a part of us. In striking contrast to this fact, we have the direct opposite stated of our Lord, and interestingly enough, it is written by John in his first Epistle:

> . . . *In Him* is *no sin.*   1 JOHN 3:5

The peculiar use of this expression in these two books suggests that they were penned by the same writer.

Another word common to the Epistle and the Gospel is the Greek word *Paraklētos,* from which we get our English word *paraclete.* It is translated "Comforter" in the Gospel (John 14:16,26; 15:26; 16:7), and "Advocate" in the Epistle (1 John 2:1). It literally signifies "one called alongside to help," "one who undertakes your cause," "a friend of the accused." In the Gospel the Comforter is the Holy Spirit, and His ministry there is to provide companionship (14:16), counsel (14:26), courage (15:26), and conviction (16:7). Thus we have the Divine Paraclete with us here to provide for us during our earthly pilgrimage. But in the Epistle where the word is translated "Advocate," the Divine Paraclete is Jesus Christ the Son, and His ministry as such is constantly to present to the Father the *satisfaction* for our sins. The usage of this one word brings the Gospel and the Epistle together as having the same author.

No one can doubt that the author of this Epistle had a close and an intimate fellowship with the Lord Jesus Christ (1:1-3). We know that there were three apostles who only were with Christ on several occasions—Peter, James, and John. They only were with Him on the Mount of Transfiguration, in the house of Jairus, and at the Garden of Gethsemane. But this Epistle does not bear the likeness of the writings of Peter and James as much as it does the writings of John.

When this Epistle was written, John was probably the only surviving apostle. The years had mellowed this disciple whom Jesus loved, the one who leaned on Christ's bosom. In this last inspired word to the Church, the author retires to the background, unwilling to speak of himself. Though we do not have the name of the penman, we can sense the dedicated personality of a humble man of God whose soul had become enriched through fellowship with the Lord Jesus Christ.

The reader must not be burdened at this time with more parallel passages in these two books, nor with other arguments. We shall meet them later on in our study of the Epistle. Suffice it to say here that the Epistle was written by the same hand that penned the fourth Gospel account.

The name *John* corresponds to the Old Testament *Jonah,* which means "a dove." John was the son of Zebedee, a fisherman on the Sea of Galilee (Mark 1:19-20; Luke 5:10), and Salome (Matthews 27:56; Mark 15:40), and was the younger brother of James (Matthew 4:21). He was no doubt influenced to Christ through the faithful preaching of John the Baptist. John became a devout follower of the Lord Jesus and a loyal witness to Christ's deity. No penman of New Testament books has set forth a Christological stamp as fully and forcefully as the Apostle John in the introductory words of his writings.

There are two principle ways of treating the theology of John. Dr. C. C. Ryrie says, "One considers all of John's writings as a unit; the other separates the Gospel and deals with it from the viewpoint of the theology of Jesus rather than the theology of John. This latter course is preferable if one's basic concept of New Testament Biblical theology is that the teachings of Jesus are its focal point from which other types of apostolic teaching emanate and evolve. To treat all of John's writings as a unit is more desirable if one prefers to emphasize the individuality of the Johannine type of thought." We concur with Dr. Ryrie if one is pursuing a course in New Testament theology, but in this series of studies we are concerned with the major emphases in the Epistles of John. A man like Moses, or John, may write five books, and in those books one would find a certain unity and similarity, but in each of the books there would be a marked individuality as well. The Bible was written by books, that is, God gave it to the human penmen, a book at a time. As a matter of fact, there is a pronounced unity and similarity in the entire Bible. Nevertheless the Bible should be studied book by book.

The first Epistle of John is one of seven shorter Epistles of the New Testament that are usually treated as a class by themselves. These are known as the general, or "catholic," Epistles, to distinguish them from the Epistles which were written to a particular church or community of believers, such as the church at Rome or the church at Philippi. The most satisfactory explanation of the term "catholic" is that which understands the Epistles of James, Peter, John, and Jude to have been addressed to a wider constituency than the Epistles of Paul. The second and third Epistles of John are addressed to individuals, and consequently are not general, or catholic, in the sense we have just stated, but at a very early date they became a part of the first Epistle, and therefore have been placed with it in this group.

This Epistle has been thought by some to have been written to a specific group of Christians, possibly those in Ephesus. This conclusion has no doubt been based upon the fact that the Gnostic heresy, which John seeks to refute, flourished in that city. But we must remember that the Gnostic heresy was quite strong at Colosse, and that it doubtless penetrated other churches in Asia as well. In that case, this Epistle would be thought of and used as a circular letter, designed to meet the needs in several churches. Chapters 2 and 3 of the Revelation show the Apostle John's connection with a number of churches in Asia Minor. There was a master heresy in all of Asia Minor, and the apostle deals with this in his first Epistle even as Paul dealt with it in his letter to the Colossians. But these matters will be considered later in our study.

It will suffice to conclude this brief introductory chapter by saying that this Epistle was written by the Apostle John, and it is doubtless the product of his advanced age. The time of the writing is about the year 90 A.D., and it is one of the latest, if not the last, books given by the Holy Spirit for the instruction and edification of the family of God.

The Gospel according to John is a record of miracles, showing the divine power, in order that sinners might be convicted (John 20:31).

The Epistles are a record of messages, showing the divine pattern, in order that the saved might be confirmed (1 John 5:13). There is not the supernatural element in miracles and visions in the Epistles.

The Book of the Revelation is a record of manifestations, setting forth divine prophecies, in order that saints might be comforted (Revelation 1:9,19).

THE FIRST EPISTLE OF JOHN

PART TWO

THE PERSONS IN THE EPISTLE

II. THE PERSONS IN THE EPISTLE

A. How the Relationship is Described
1 John 1:2,3
1 John 2:1,12,13,15,16,18,22,23,24,28
1 John 3:1,7,18
1 John 4:4,14
1 John 5:7,21

B. How the Relationship is Determined
1 John 2:29
1 John 3:9
1 John 4:7,8,16
1 John 5:1,4,5,18

That this Epistle is addressed to believers will be obviously clear once we have examined such terms as "Father," "little children," and "born." These terms express the relationship to God of the persons addressed. Upon examining them we see both a description and a definition of this relationship.

A. *How the Relationship is Described.*

The word *father* (Greek, *pater*) is used as the originator of a family, the members of which possess the same nature and are motivated by the same spirit as the father himself. Here in First John the "Father" is God, and the word is used of that relationship between Him and those who have been born again by His Spirit. The word "Father" appears

20

no less than thirteen times (1:2,3; 2:1,13,15,16,22,23,24; 3:1; 4:14; 5:7).

John's use of the word refutes the false theory of the universal fatherhood of God. Quoting our Lord's words to the Pharisees, he wrote: "I speak that which I have seen with *My Father:* and ye do that which ye have seen with *your father....* Ye do the deeds of *your father....* Ye are of *your father* the devil, and the lusts of *your father* ye will do" (John 8:38,41,44). The scriptural teaching of the fatherhood of God is not a part of the doctrine of creation, as some argue from Paul's sermon at Mars' Hill. It is true that all men are the offspring of God in a creative sense, for the apostle said, "God . . . hath made of one blood all nations. . . . For we are also His offspring" (Acts 17:24,26, 28). But so are the birds, fishes, and animals the *offspring* (Greek, *genos*) of God, that is, they all had their origin with Him. Fatherhood means more than the ultimate source of man in creation. Jesus told the religious Pharisees of His day that the devil was their father, but still they were God's offspring in creation. When writing to the churches in the province of Galatia, Paul said, "For ye are all the children of God by faith in Christ Jesus" (Galatians 3:26).

The persons to whom this Epistle is written are called "little children." This term appears not less than eight times (1 John 2:1,12,18,28; 3:7,18; 4:4; 5:21). It is not a term expressing immaturity as in chapter 2:13 where "little children" is used in contrast to the fathers and young men. It is the Greek word *teknia,* a term of endearment used to express the spiritual relationship between the Father and His children. It is sometimes translated *dear children* and *born ones.* In Scotland a mother might refer to her own children as "my bairns" [my born ones]. It gives prominence to the fact of birth as illustrated in John 1:12-13.

The birth here is a spiritual one, wrought supernaturally in the believing sinner by the Holy Spirit (John 3:3-8). The use of "my" here in 1 John 2:1 and 3:18 does not imply that John looked upon those to whom he wrote as his spiritual children in the sense that Paul considered Timothy to be his son in the faith (1 Timothy 1:2; 2 Timothy 2:2). Rather the apostle uses it to address those who are the children of God, *His* born ones, *His* dear children. Christ used the term "little children" when addressing His disciples after Judas slipped out into the dark to betray Him (John 13:33). John heard our Lord use it on that occasion, and remembering how He dealt with His disciples, he would now deal with believers after the same fashion. Paul employed it in his Epistle to the Galatians long before John wrote his books (Galatians 4:19).

In this Epistle the term "little children" is more than a mark of identification; it is an appeal to the new man in Christ, an appeal to the highest and holiest that is in him. It is used here to draw believers together into a realization of their partnership with God and with one another. Their spiritual development depended somewhat upon their appreciation of this relationship. First John has been called the *sanctum sanctorum* of the New Testament, taking the believer across the threshhold into the fellowship of the Father and His family. It is the "family" Epistle. Though it might have been written with the churches of Asia Minor in mind, its broader application is to all Christians of this entire Church Age, the one true Church, Christ's Body, made up of God's children.

B. *How the Relationship is Determined.*

The children of God, those who have God as their Father, have become such through being born again. The apostle uses the word "born" seven times in this Epistle, each usage bringing to light one of the birthmarks of the born-again ones.

The first birthmark of God's children is the practice of righteousness.

> *If ye know that He is righteous, ye know that every one that doeth righteousness is born of Him.*
>
> 1 JOHN 2:29

Someone may argue that there are plenty of morally good persons in the world who, even though they are not born again, do righteousness. But such reasoning misses the meaning and bearing of the verse. The "righteousness" here is God's righteousness in contradistinction to man's righteousness. The two are as different as night is from day. That which man calls righteousness is as a polluted garment in God's eyes (Isaiah 64:6). There is that righteousness which the Bible calls "the righteousness of God" (Romans 1:17; 3:5,21,25,26). The unsaved are totally ignorant of it, and "being ignorant of God's righteousness, and going about to establish their own righteousness, have not submitted themselves unto the righteousness of God" (Romans 10:3). God's righteousness is an attribute peculiar to Himself, and it means essentially the same as His faithfulness, His truthfulness—that quality of holiness in Him which must find expression in His hatred and condemnation of sin. Man's standard of righteousness falls far below God's. It is only as one is in Christ that he becomes a "new creation" [is born again], and thus becomes "the righteousness of God in Him" (2 Corinthians 5:17,21). It is only in Christ that a man can become all that God requires him to be, and then righteousness is reckoned to him because of his faith in Christ (Romans 4:6,11), "not by works of righteousness which we have done" (Titus 3:5). The man who is born again seeks first the kingdom of God and *His* righteousness (Matthew 6:33).

The Apostle John is saying in 1 John 2:29 that he who doeth righteousness is born of God, because God's nature has become his nature. The reality of one's sonship may be deduced from the fact that God's righteousness abides in him. Internally, the right relationship to God is acquired through faith, but an outward expression of righteousness in the life is the way of determining whether or not one has been born again. Test yourself! The conclusive evidence of your relationship to God is your standard of righteousness. Doing and thinking righteously is the normal expression of, yea, the proof of, the new birth. It is a righteousness which comes from being right. The tense of the verb "doeth" denotes the habitual doing of God's will, for, after all, it is the habitual actions of a person that are an index to his character.

Further light is shed upon the meaning of our verse on examining the word *know*. It appears twice. The first *know* (Greek, *oida*), means to have seen or perceived either intuitively or from observation. The second *know* (Greek, *ginōskō*) means to know experientially. Knowledge possessed through the intellectual process of learning is one thing; knowledge gained by experience, by an active relationship between the one who knows and the person or thing known, is far superior to the former.

The next appearance of the word "born" (3:9), along with that in 5:18, we shall study in the following section of the book where we take up the purposes in writing the Epistle. Looking now at chapter 4:7, we see another birthmark of the born-again ones.

Beloved, let us love one another: for love is of God; and every one that loveth is born of God, and knoweth God. 1 JOHN 4:7

Christianity is preeminently a religion of love. It had its
origin in the love of God (John 3:16; Romans 5:8). God
in His essence is love (1 John 4:8,16). Love is that eternal
attribute of God wherein He is moved to communicate
Himself to man, in man's behalf, regardless of any sacrifice
on His own part. He is called "the God of love" (2 Corinthians 13:11).

Being born again is the equivalent of becoming a partaker of God's nature (2 Peter 1:4), and since God is love,
our new birth brings with it the seed of divine love. "The
love of God is shed abroad in our hearts by the Holy
Ghost which is given unto us" (Romans 5:5).

Since God is the source of love, John is saying that the
mutual love of believers is evidence that they are the children of God. To exhibit divine love is a proof of an in-
creasing experiential knowledge of God, for:

He that loveth not knoweth not God; for God is love.
1 JOHN 4:8

This statement, "knoweth not God," includes the absence of the new birth. The exhortation to "love one another" speaks of continuous action, as though God were
saying, "Let us be habitually loving one another." It is a
reciprocal love which can be demonstrated only by the
"beloved" [the divinely-loved ones]. As the "little children" are in fellowship with the "Father," a perpetual
stream of love flows from Him to us, thus from us to each
other. The ground of our love to the brethren is not in
ourselves, but in Him who loveth us with His own pure
love. If we love God who gave us our new birth, we will
love him also that is begotten [born] of God (5:1). Since
every child of God shares in the gift of divine life by which
he is born of God, it is inevitable that the love life will be
manifested likewise to those who are born of God.

In concluding this study, in which we have attempted
to identify the persons addressed in the Epistle, we shall
look at one more verse in which the word "born" appears.

> *For whatsoever is born of God overcometh the
> world: and this is the victory that overcometh the
> world, even our faith.* 1 JOHN 5:4

Who are the "born of God"? They are those who have
been begotten by God, who have had imparted to them
by God His own nature. They are those upon whom He
has conferred the disposition of "children."

From the very moment of this regenerating experience,
which commenced in faith (as far as we are concerned),
there has been available to us the power necessary for victory over the world. We are not expected to fight all over
again the battle that Christ has already won for us. He
said, "Be of good cheer; I have overcome the world" (John
16:33). As we commenced our new life in faith, trusting
in Christ's redeeming *work,* so we continue walking by
faith, trusting His revealed *Word.* The victory we win day
by day is nothing more or less than our appropriation of
the victory our Lord gained once for all.

The power of this world system is not to be underesti-
mated. Its manifold temptations are to be reckoned with.
The Christian in the world is in a conflict. The word
victory (Greek, *nikē*) occurs here only in the New Testament, and it speaks of the conquest that God's children
can experience day by day through faith. The opposition
which causes us trouble is already overcome. He who continues to overcome, to conquer, is he who appropriates the
victory already won. The shield of faith, then, is the armor
that assures victory (Ephesians 6:16). It is not the mere
wearing of the armor occasionally but continually, so that
faith develops and grows through life's stages and crises.

The birthmark of the born-again ones is a habit of life to gain victory in the warfare against the world, the flesh, and the devil. To experience defeat is the exception, not the rule. The "little children" are in permanent possession of the power to overcome the world. The secret to victorious living is, first, to be born and, then, to believe. Three times in 1 John 5:4,5 we read the phrase, "overcometh the world." It is addressed to those who are "born of God." The new birth gives us the potential of a new faith, which in turn makes possible new victories every day. There is no other way of overcoming the world except through the new birth and a new belief.

Who is he that overcometh the world, but he that believeth that Jesus is the Son of God?   1 JOHN 5:5

THE FIRST EPISTLE OF JOHN

Part Three

THE PURPOSES OF THE EPISTLE

III. TO PROFFER FELLOWSHIP

A. The Principle of Fellowship
    1 John 1:3

B. The Participation in the Fellowship
    1 John 1:1,3
    1 John 2:22-24
    1 John 4:2,3,15
    1 John 5:1,7,10-12,20

C. The Pretence of Fellowship
    1 John 1:5,6,7,8,10
    1 John 2:6,11
    1 John 3:10

D. The Practice of Fellowship
    1 John 1:3,6,7

That which we have seen and heard declare we unto you, that ye also may have fellowship with us: and truly our fellowship is with the Father, and with His Son Jesus Christ. 1 JOHN 1:3

The thought here is a continuation of verse 1. (Note that verse two is in parentheses.) The first of the purposes for which the Epistle was written is that the reader might enjoy true Christian fellowship. This word "fellowship" appears four times in the first chapter, and it is one of the most important words in this letter.

A. *The Principle of Fellowship.*

The English word *fellowship,* as it is used today, usually means "friendly, social intercourse." This is not what John had in mind, however. At the time he wrote this general letter to be sent to the Church at large, he was an old man, and certainly had no thought of ever sitting down to enjoy a season of mere friendly, social intercourse with his readers. This commonly accepted usage of the word could not have been first in the aged apostle's thoughts.

The word used here means *partnership.* When two or more persons share something in common, they are said to be partakers or partners together. The partnership of which John writes here is, first, a partnership with God the Father, for he says, *"truly our fellowship [partnership] is with the Father"* (1:3). Men get up their social fellowships, but the true Christian fellowship is a partnership in the gospel of Christ (Philippians 1:5). No individual can share in it until he becomes a *partaker* of God's nature in regeneration. The new birth is the believing sinner's initiation into a brand-new partnership with deity.

The Apostle Peter uses the same word to describe the new birth when he says, "Whereby are given unto us exceeding great and precious promises: that by these ye might be *partakers* of the divine nature, having escaped the corruption that is in the world through lust" (2 Peter 1:4). The new fellowship begins here and now; it grows as we give ourselves more and more to it; and it has its final consummation in the life to come. To the extent to which we are partners in Christ's sufferings, we shall share as partners in His glory. "But rejoice, inasmuch as ye are *partakers* of Christ's sufferings; that, when His glory shall be revealed, ye may be glad also with exceeding joy" (1 Peter 4:13). "The elders which are among you I exhort,

who am also an elder, and a witness of the sufferings of
Christ, and also a *partaker* of the glory that shall be revealed" (1 Peter 5:1). Paul seemingly had in mind the
future partnership with Christ in His glory, when he wrote,
"That I may know Him, and the power of His resurrection,
and the *fellowship* [partnership] of His sufferings, being
made conformable unto His death" (Philippians 3:10). He
knew that those saints who would take up the cross, and
gladly be partakers in its shame and suffering, will have a
larger share in the life to come. Thus he exhorted Timothy,
"Be not thou therefore ashamed of the testimony of our
Lord, nor of me His prisoner: but be thou *partaker* of the
afflictions of the gospel according to the power of God"
(2 Timothy 1:8), for "If we suffer, we shall also reign with
Him" (2 Timothy 2:12).

B. *The Participation in the Fellowship.*

Now observe next that the partnership with Deity is a
joint partnership with the Father and the Son. *"Truly our
fellowship is with the Father, and with His Son Jesus
Christ."* In this statement the Holy Spirit continues His
argument for the deity of our Lord Jesus Christ. He is the
eternal "Word" (1 John 1:1) who was *"with God"* and who
"was God" (John 1:1), and without whom no man can
have fellowship with God. Men may talk and preach and
write about God, but it is impossible to have communion
with Him apart from His Son, Jesus Christ. This point is
made with double emphasis in First John (2:22-24; 4:2,3,15;
5:1,7,10-12,20). God wants partners, companions, but He
will not have anyone as His partner and companion who
refuses to enter into partnership with His Son. John alludes
to this in his only use of the word *"bosom."* In the beginning of John's Gospel account Christ is seen in the Father's

bosom, a term used to express His eternal and essential relationship with the Father (John 1:18). At the end of the record, John is found leaning on Jesus' *bosom* (John 13:23), showing us where the Father would have us be if we would have fellowship with Him. (See 1 Corinthians 1:9.)

This was the *fellowship* into which the apostles had been brought through Christ (1:1), and which John now desires to share with the Church.

That which we have seen and heard declare we unto you, that ye also may have fellowship with us. . . .
1 JOHN 1:3

John wants that which they saw and heard and experienced about Christ to be the common possession of all believers. He desired to communicate to them, contribute to them, distribute among them, those deeper truths and precious experiences of our blessed Lord. Such a *fellowship* is Christianity at its best.

Though this partnership with God and with one another is basically a spiritual one, it extends to practical matters as well. The same Greek word [*koinonia*] is rendered *contribution* in Romans 15:26; *distribution* in 2 Corinthians 9:13; and *communication* in Hebrews 13:16. The thought is the same in all three words, connoting the idea of sharing what we have with others (Acts 4:35), as when Christ "distributed" the five loaves and two fishes (John 6:11); and Paul admonished the believers with the words, "distributing to the necessity of the saints" (Romans 12:13). A Christian brother, with whom I correspond, signs his letters "Yours because His." And that just about sums up in a sentence this blessed fellowship with the Godhead and with each other.

C. *The Pretence of Fellowship.*

It is important at this point that we consider verses 6
and 7, where we have the only other appearance of the
word "fellowship" in the Epistle.

> *If we say that we have fellowship with Him, and*
> *walk in darkness, we lie, and do not the truth.*
>
> 1 JOHN 1:6

In order to bring out the forcefulness of the modes and
tenses of this passage in its original language, I am passing
on to you a translation by the late Dr. H. Framer Smith.
It reads: "Should ever we actually say that we are certainly
partnershiping with Him and (at the same time) in the
skotos [darkness] should be walking about, we certainly
are deceiving ourselves and are certainly not practicing the
truth."

The neuter noun *skotos* [darkness] is used only twice by
John in his five books, here in 1 John 1:6 and in John 3:19.
Metaphorically the word is used of moral and spiritual
darkness, the darkness of sin. Fellowshiping with God and
walking about in darkness are mutually exclusive experiences. The one who pretends to be doing so is a liar and
is not practicing the truth. Like Judas, we are in great danger of being in the constant presence of the Light, yet all
the while walking in darkness. And be certain that our
pretending will one day be exposed. "Therefore judge
nothing before the time, until the Lord come, who both
will bring to light the hidden things of darkness, and will
make manifest the counsels of the hearts: and then shall
every man have praise of God" (1 Corinthians 4:5).

Our Lord said to His disciples, "Ye are the light of the
world. . . . Let your light so shine before men, that they
may see your good works, and glorify your Father which is

in heaven" (Matthew 5:14,16). Paul added, "For ye were sometimes darkness, but now are ye light in the Lord: walk as children of light" (Ephesians 5:8). John says, "God is Light" (1 John 1:5). Christ said, "I am the Light of the world" (John 8:12). Light is the emblem of holiness. It is what God is. Satan's kingdom is a kingdom of darkness, of moral and spiritual evil (Ephesians 6:12). Our regeneration in Christ transferred us out of Satan's dark kingdom into the kingdom of God (Colossians 1:13), who has called us out of darkness into His marvelous light (1 Peter 2:9). Light and darkness have nothing in common; therefore he is a liar who walks in darkness and pretends to be in fellowship with the Light. We may be self-deceived or we may be hypocrites. At any rate, there is base inconsistency where outward profession is contrary to inward reality. One of God's first acts in creation was illumination, dividing the light from the darkness (Genesis 1:3-4), and it must ever be so. The two have no mutual existence at one and the same place (2 Corinthians 6:14).

The apostle then makes the distinction between our *words* and our *walk*. Three allegations, all lies, are prefaced with the words, "If we *say*" (1:6,8,10). The first lie (verse 6) is that of the one whose words indicate that he is in communion with God, but whose walk refutes his words. In his first letter John mentions four times the believer's walk (1:6,7; 2:6,11). Socrates and Aristotle were known as *peripatetic* teachers, men who taught their students as they walked about the Lyceum near Athens. How are we walking about? If we keep in mind that by our walk we instruct others, we will walk in newness of life (Romans 6:4), honestly (Romans 13:12-13), by faith (2 Corinthians 5:7), in the Spirit (Galatians 5:16), in love (Ephesians 5:2), circumspectly (Ephesians 5:15). The walk of a man is the distinguishing characteristic which differentiates the children of

God from the children of the devil (1 John 3:10). There is a terrible indictment upon the hypocrite, of whom Paul writes, "They profess that they know God; but in works they deny Him, being abominable, and disobedient, and unto every good work reprobate" (Titus 1:16).

D. *The Practice of Fellowship.*

But if we walk in the light, as He is in the light, we have fellowship one with another, and the blood of Jesus Christ His Son cleanseth us from all sin.

1 JOHN 1:7

In the use of "we" here, believers only are included, for there first must be union before communion. This verse is not an easy one to interpret. Two questions confront us. First, what is meant by the phrase, "the blood of Jesus Christ cleanseth [goes on cleansing] us from all sin"? Is this a positional cleansing; that is, does the blood shed at Calvary, by which we are justified (Romans 3:24), maintain our standing before God? Or does the text mean that the believer is being saved presently from the power and practice of sins? I believe it is the former. Cleansing from the power and practice of sins comes through our knowledge of, and obedience to, the Word of God (John 17:17). The fellowship here is our joint partnership with God, and His with us. When we walk in the light of God's own holy nature and pure truth, we are in fellowship with Him. Thank God for all who walk in the light of God's countenance (Psalm 89:15). They are not only in the family, but are enjoying the fellowship as well. Having been justified once through faith in Christ's blood, the blood goes on cleansing us from all sin—sins of omission, sins of ignorance, even sins we have committed and did not recognize as sin because we had not grown sufficiently to detect them as sin.

The second question here has to do with the "we" in the phrase, *"we* have fellowship one with another." To whom does the pronoun "we" refer? Does it mean that Christians have fellowship one with another, or that God and the Christian have fellowship one with another? I believe the context indicates the fellowship is between God and the Christian. In verse 6 it is "fellowship with Him." Actually in verse 6 we see who does *not* have fellowship with God, while in verse 7 we are shown who *does* have fellowship with Him. Now it is true that believers, walking in the light, do have fellowship with one another, but that fellowship must be predicated upon the fact that they are in fellowship with the Father and the Son (1:3).

Summing up the contents of this chapter, we see in the *koinonia* a sixfold fellowship:

> The Fellowship of Salvation—2 Peter 1:4
> The Fellowship of the Spirit—Philippians 2:1
> The Fellowship of the Saints—1 John 1:3
> The Fellowship of our Substance—Romans 12:13; 15:26; 2 Corinthians 9:13; Philippians 4:14,15
> The Fellowship of Christ's Sufferings—Philippians 3:10; 2 Timothy 1:8; 1 Peter 4:13
> The Fellowship of Christ's Sovereignty—2 Timothy 2:12; 1 Peter 5:1

IV. TO PROMOTE JOY

1 John 1:3,6,7,8,9,10

And these things write we unto you, that your joy may be full.   1 JOHN 1:4

The order here is proper. There can be no real joy until the partnership with God and His Son and His children has been established. When our fellowship is what it ought to be, the attainment of the fullness of joy will result. If you ask by what means this joy can be realized, I can only repeat what I have just said: namely, make certain your fellowship remains unbroken. The joy is always present wherever the fellowship is preserved.

This verse contains the only appearance of the word "joy" in First John. It is the Greek word *chara,* translated *delight, gladness.* It is a feeling of pleasurable emotion and exultation caused by the expectation or the realization of some good thing. An illustration of joy caused by the expectation of something good is the announcement of our Lord's birth in Luke 2:10. Two illustrations of joy caused by that which already has happened are the saints Paul led to Christ at Philippi, resulting in his joy (Philippians 4:1), and those likewise at Thessalonica (1 Thessalonians 2:19-20).

It was our Lord's desire for His own that they have glad hearts. This was one of His goals in instructing them (John 15:11). He told them that prayer was an aid to achieving it (John 16:24), and He prayed to the Father that He might give it to them (John 17:13). The only true source of such delight and gladness is in the Lord (Isaiah 29:19; 41:15-16; Habakkuk 3:17-18. We must beware of disunity, because it is a destroyer of joy (Philippians 4:1-4).

Some grounds of Christian joy are: the power of God (Acts 8:5-8); the presence of Christ (John 16:22; 20:20); the prospect of reward (Matthew 5:12; Luke 6:23); the preaching of the gospel (Philippians 1:18); the prosperity of other believers (Romans 12:15; 2 Corinthians 7:13,16).

In the First Epistle of John joy is promoted through fellowship (1:3,6,7); fidelity (1:6,8,10); full assurance (the word "know" is used 38 times); the faithfulness of God (1:9).

Let us examine our text (1:4) more closely. *"These things"* points to the whole Epistle itself, written to believers in order that their joy might be perfected. Each of us goes through periods of joy caused by circumstances or conditions, but here the goal is toward something higher than a mere up-today-and-down-tomorrow experience. The *joy* here is a consummate and constant thing at all times and under every condition. (See Acts 5:41 and 2 Corinthians 8:2.) Archbishop Leighton said, "It is a paradox to the world that there is a joy which can subsist in the midst of sorrow, that the saints have not only some measure of joy in the griefs that abound upon them here, but excellent and eminent joy." This is blessedly true, and it is true only because Christ Himself, who indwells the Christian, is the perfect example of it. "Looking unto Jesus, the author and finisher of our faith; who for the *joy* that was set before Him endured the cross" (Hebrews 12:2).

The joy that was set before our Lord was the doing of the Father's will and the anticipation of the glory that would follow. In this He is our example and encouragement. Thus He said to His disciples, "These things have

I spoken unto you, that My *joy* might remain in you, and
that your *joy* might be full" (John 15:11). What are "these
things"? Look at the preceding verse. "If ye keep My
commandments, ye shall abide in My love; even as I have
kept My Father's commandments, and abide in His love."
He is stating simply that the keeping of the Father's commandments is His joy, and that the joy of His followers
would reach its highest point in their obedience to the
Word of God. The foundation of a permanent, continuous, and full joy is in our yielding to God's will as set forth
in His Word.

None of us need to have proved to us that disobedience
takes the joy out of our lives. David learned this bitter
lesson. When he repented of his sin he cried to God, "Restore unto me the joy of Thy salvation" (Psalm 51:12).
When he sinned he lost the joy he received when he became saved. Now he prays for cleansing (verse 2) and
purification (verse 7), and then for the joy which follows
such cleansing (verses 8,12). He had been hearing about
the judgment of God on his sins, but with forgiveness and
cleansing he would have joy and gladness once again. Once
we have lost our joy because of sin, nothing save God's forgiveness and cleansing can restore it. Such restoration is
compared to the setting of broken bones and restoring them
again to strength (verse 8). So pronounced was the absence
of joy in this sinning saint, that he prayed to God both to
restore the joy and to preserve him lest he sin and lose
it again. Confession paves the way for cleansing and forgiveness, and this in turn leaves the way clear for the
restoration of lost joy.

One of the lamentations of Jeremiah, as he beheld the
woes of his people and the desolations of the holy city,
was, "The joy of our heart is ceased; our dance is turned
into mourning" (Lamentations 5:15). There was heaviness

in the prophet's heart and exercise of his soul as he re-
flected upon the past sins of the people and the present
judgment of God. One of those judgments was the re-
placement of the joyful note of the singer with the doleful
dirge of the mourner. Gunkel called the Book of Lamentations, "The political funeral song." A Roman coin, com-
memorating the city's destruction by Titus in A.D. 70, shows
her as a dejected and defeated woman sitting under a
palm tree, and bearing the inscription *Judaea capta*—
"Judah is gone into captivity" (Lamentations 1:3). The
awful retribution of God, which the people brought upon
themselves because of their transgression, was one of great
sorrow and affliction and loss of joy. They said, "The joy
of our heart is ceased."

"My joy . . . in you." Our Lord intends His people to be
the possessors of His joy, a joy that is exhibited in the face
of the most ignominious shame and suffering. Commenting
on this text, J. Sidlow Baxter said, "Away with sepulchral
sanctimoniousness! A religion which wears graveclothes
begs to be buried, and the sooner the funeral the better!
Jesus came to give joy. Mere 'religion' may be sombre and
dowdy, but true Christianity is more than a religion, it is
new life in Christ Jesus—and this new life is a life of joy."

The context in John 15 makes it quite plain as to just
how we may have His own joy at all times and under
every circumstance. It is by our *union* and *communion*
with Christ. This is the truth expressed by the metaphor
of the vine and the branches, and taught clearly by the
words, "abide in Me . . . abide in the Vine . . . abide in
Me" (verse 4), "abideth in Me" (verse 5), "abide in Me"
(verse 7). When we are abiding in Christ, there is uninterrupted communion, thus an uninterrupted flow of His
joy, the same kind of joy He exhibited at all times.

"These things" in our Lord's words in John 15:11 are

the same things as *"these things"* in John's statement in 1 John 1:4, only expressed differently. In the former it is stated in terms of abiding and obeying; in the latter in terms of fellowshiping. The religion of Christianity is one of joy because it is one of fellowship with Christ, in whose "presence is fulness of joy" (Psalm 16:11). Joy is the blessed fruit of the Spirit (Galatians 5:22). Nothing was more characteristic of the first Christians than the fullness of joy, a joy which is not given to the ungodly. It is of such a nature that it cannot be lost in the darkest hour.

All Christian joy is based on the finished work of Christ. Salvation and joy are linked together. The angel announced the coming of the Saviour with the words, "Behold, I bring you good tidings of great joy" (Luke 2:10). When the eunuch was saved and was baptized, "he went on his way rejoicing" (Acts 8:39). When the jailer was saved, he "rejoiced, believing in God with all his house" (Acts 16:34). When Philip preached Christ in Samaria, and many believed, "There was great joy in that city" (Acts 8:8). Have you ever noticed the gloom and sadness attached to all religions outside of Christianity? In Christ only can one "rejoice with joy unspeakable and full of glory" (1 Peter 1:8). Joy in Christ is much different from the hollow happiness of this world. "Blessed is the people that know the joyful sound" (Psalm 89:15).

V. TO PREVENT SIN

A. The Principle of Sin
    1 John 1:6,7,8,9,10
    1 John 2:1,2,12
    1 John 3:4,5,6,8,9
    1 John 4:10
    1 John 5:16,17,18

B. The Prohibition of Sin
    1 John 2:1,8
    1 John 3:6,9
    1 John 5:18

C. The Provision for Sin
    1 John 2:1,2
    1 John 3:5
    1 John 4:10

D. The Penalty for Sin
    1 John 1:9
    1 John 5:16

My little children, these things write I unto you, that ye sin not. And if any man sin, we have an advocate with the Father, Jesus Christ the righteous: And He is the propitiation for our sins: and not for ours only, but also for the sins of the whole world.

                        1 JOHN 2:1-2

The subject of sin is prominent in this Epistle. In the noun and verb forms combined, the word "sin" appears not less than twenty-eight times, not including the words "unrighteousness," "wicked," and "evil" (1:7,8,9,10; 2:1,12; 3:4,5,6,8,9; 4:10; 5:16,17,18). It is in the Father's heart that His children know precisely, not presumably, the meaning of sin and its fearful and fatal results. The varied usages of the word in the Epistle provide a well-rounded course of study on the subject.

A. *The Principle of Sin.*

At times the word is used in the generic sense as virtually equivalent to a condition.

> *If we say that we have no sin, we deceive ourselves,*
> *and the truth is not in us.*   1 JOHN 1:8

Here, as in John 1:29, where we find the expression "the sin [not sins] of the world," the singular is used to show sin in its unity as the common corruption of all humanity. To deny the fact of sin is a false assertion. We know this even though we persuade ourselves that sin is not present. I interpret the expression in this verse to mean original sin, a condition from which the committing of sins proceeds.

We stated in the introductory chapter that the phrase "have no sin," which is peculiar to John's writings, refers to the sin principle in all men. It had its entrance into the human race through "one man" (Romans 5:12), by "one man's offence" (Romans 5:17), and because of "one man's disobedience" (Romans 5:19). That one man was Adam, and by virtue of the solidarity of the human race, all men have inherited from Adam the nature of sin and therefore the tendency to commit acts of sin. The record of human history proves this. The condition of sin is uni-

versal at all times. The birth of every baby in the world
marks the entrance of another sinner on the stage of human
experience. It is heresy to say that we have not the principle of sin in us, to deny the indwelling, totally depraved
nature passed on to all mankind from Adam. The Scripture says of such a person that the truth is not in him.
The one exception is our Lord Jesus Christ, of whom it is
written, "In Him is no sin" (1 John 3:5).

There are two definitions of sin in the Epistle. (1) *"Sin
is the transgression of the law"* (3:4). In the Greek text the
words, *the transgression of the law,* are one word, *anoinia,*
meaning "lawlessness." Sin and lawlessness are the same.
Any violation of any part of divine law is sin (James 2:10),
and that law has a threefold relation: to God, to others,
and to ourselves. This lawlessness extends beyond the Ten
Commandments, for there was sin in the world before ever
God gave the written law at Sinai. Roy L. Laurin has said,
"This makes it more than a legal problem. It is a life
problem." (2) *"All unrighteousness is sin"* (5:17). Everything that is not right according to God's standard is sin.
Any unrighteous thought, word, or deed is a manifestation
of sin. So then, whether in the disposition to set law aside,
as in chapter 3:4, or in these of unfair, unjust, and unkind
words and deeds, we have sinned because we are sinners
by nature.

Verse 8 is a warning to the "little children" never to conclude that the sin nature can be eradicated in this life.
Paul testified that everything in his life that went wrong
was the result of "sin that dwelleth in me" (Romans 7:17).
The Christian is no longer in sin, but sin is still in him.
To deny the existence of impulses and affections of sensual
desires, at least in the intellectual or thought life, is to
deceive oneself. Such an one has been led into error and
falsehood. Against his better knowledge, in spiritual pride,

he has erred who sinks into an evasion of the pronounced existing condition of sin. In this we neither deceive God nor our friends, but we do deceive ourselves. Just as the walker in darkness cannot claim fellowship with God (1:6), no more can the walker in light claim that he does not possess sin. Walking in the light, we know that the sin principle is a continuous source of influence upon us. If we deny this we lead ourselves astray and we are responsible for it. Beware of pseudoperfectionism!

The warning continues in 1 John 1:10:

> *If we say that we have not sinned, we make Him a liar, and His word is not in us.*

In verse 8, we had the denial of the indwelling principle of sin. In this verse, we have the denial of the practice of sins. Kenneth S. Wuest says: "The verb is in the perfect tense, which tense in Greek refers to an action completed in past time, having present results. The denial here is of any acts of sin committed in past time with the implication that none are able to be committed at present. This is sinless perfection with a vengeance." Such a foolish assumption is an imposition and impiety against God. It is so blasphemous that we make God Himself a sinner.

While every born-again one stands pardoned through Christ's blood, it is good for us to remember, and not deny, our former iniquities. David remembered his transgressions (Psalm 51:3). So did Paul (Galatians 1:13; 1 Timothy 1:15). We may rejoice daily in our unalterable position in Christ, but to remember that we were sinners, and that those sins we committed in the past we can commit again, will keep us mindful that we are debtors to God's grace and that our dependence is upon Him. It will stimulate us to a deeper devotion to our Lord. It will promote watch-

fulness, exercise a spirit of repentance and faith, and cultivate holiness.

B. *The Prohibition of Sin.*

> *My little children, these things write I unto you,*
> *that ye sin not. . . .* 1 JOHN 2:1

We have just seen that the principle of sin in the believer
makes it possible for him to commit sin. And yet he is
told to "sin not." The principle and possibility of sin is
present, but the practice of sins is prohibited. This is a
strange paradox to some, and it becomes even more con-
fusing to those already confused when they read a verse
such as the following:

> *Whosoever abideth in Him sinneth not: whosoever*
> *sinneth hath not seen Him, neither known Him.*
> 1 JOHN 3:6

In this verse there are two present tenses not to be over-
looked. The first verb in the present tense is *"abideth."*
To abide means to obey (John 15:10). If you are obeying
you are abiding, and if you are abiding you are obeying.
The second verb in the present tense is *"sinneth not."* The
tense of both verbs means a continuous, habitual action.
Every one who continuously and habitually abides in Him
will not continuously and habitually keep on sinning. The
text does not deny that a Christian ever commits an act of
sin, but it does deny that a Christian sins habitually. Whosoever keeps on continually sinning has neither seen Him
with the eye of faith nor known Him in experiential salvation. What is implied here is a ruling principle of life.
To continue to abide in Christ and to continue to practice
sin are incongruous. The practice of sin excludes any professed knowledge of Christ (Matthew 7:21-22).

There is present in the Epistle a second verse which seemingly contradicts the fact of the existing condition of sin.

Whosoever is born of God doth not commit sin; for His seed remaineth in him: and he cannot sin, because he is born of God.   1 JOHN 3:9

Two things are affirmed here—"doth not commit sin" and "he cannot sin." Who is it that doeth no sin and cannot sin? That which is "born" or begotten of God. If you are born of God you have God's nature in you (2 Peter 1:4). The divine nature in every child of God is just the same as it is in Christ. Christ was born of God, and because He escaped the sin principle through His supernatural conception apart from a human father, He neither did sin nor could He sin. It is wrong to say that Christ did not sin but could have sinned if He liked. The fact of the matter is He *could not* sin. The nature of God is so abhorrent to sin, that it is impossible for Him to have any participation with it. You could no more get Christ to sin than you could contaminate the sun by the stagnant water on which it shines. Christ not only *did not* sin, but He *could not* sin.

Here is one difference between Christ and the Christian. Christ had one nature only; the Christian has two natures. When we became partakers of the divine nature, the old sin nature was not eradicated. The old nature remains unchanged, just as bad as ever, unalterable and unmended. But then too, the divine nature, His Seed, which is Christ Himself, remains unchanged and cannot sin. The word *seed* is used metaphorically of spiritual offspring, but it also signifies the principle of spiritual life imparted to the believer, and which remains in him unaltered and unalterable. Whenever I as a man, a Christian, commit an act of sin, it is the prompting of the old nature, and no

Christian can say that he does not possess the old nature, for,

> *If we say that we have no sin, we deceive ourselves, and the truth is not in us.* 1 JOHN 1:8

It is the new nature that does not sin because it cannot sin. If the believer in Christ had Christ's nature only, he never would sin. First John 3:9 holds no warrant for the erroneous teaching of sinless perfection.

Another verse in the Epistle that has caused no little difficulty is in chapter 5.

> *We know that whosoever is born of God sinneth not; but he that is begotten of God keepeth himself, and that wicked one toucheth him not.* 1 JOHN 5:18

The Christian is in view here, the one who has been begotten by the divine operation of the Holy Spirit. It is the born-again one that "sinneth not." The verb is in the present continuous tense, and it does not refer to the committing of an act of sin but rather a continuous course of sin.

The person referred to is the one who "was begotten," "not the well-meaning, not the hard-trier, not the new-leafer, but the really regenerate one," as stated by the late Guy King. Such an one will not pursue the habit of sinning. There may be the isolated or occasional act of sin, but not the course of life we lived when we "walked according to the course of this world, according to the prince of the power of the air, the spirit that now worketh in the children of disobedience" (Ephesians 2:2).

The Christian may at sometime commit sin, but he will not continue on in it. Why? First, because he has been begotten [born] of God. Secondly, he *"keepeth himself,"* not in the sense of preserving or maintaining his salvation through his own strength, but rather "to take care of, to watch over, to guard." Our Lord said, "Watch and pray, that ye enter not into temptation: the spirit indeed is willing, but the flesh is weak" (Matthew 26:41). "Endeavouring to keep [guard] the unity of the Spirit in the bond of peace" (Ephesians 4:3). The true child of God will go all out to prevent sins from getting into his life.

> *My little children, these things write I unto you, that ye sin not.*   1 JOHN 2:1

While the principle of sin in the believer is admitted, he is prohibited from sinning. *"Sin not,"* says the Holy Spirit. This is the Christian's ideal and it denies the lie which says that sinning is a necessity to the life of the child of God.

C. *The Provision for Sin.*

> *. . . And if any man sin, we have an advocate with the Father, Jesus Christ the righteous: And He is the propitiation for our sins: and not for ours only, but also for the sins of the whole world.*   1 JOHN 2:1-2

Notice that it is not an advocate "with God," but an advocate "with the *Father.*" The question between God and the believer about sin has been settled. It has been settled judicially, legally, and righteously once for all.

The sin being dealt with here is the sin of a child of God, any act of sin which breaks the fellowship between God and one of His children. It is the occasional sin of the Christian that is in view.

Now when he sins, he has an "advocate with the Father." The word *advocate* is the Greek term, *paraklētos*, translated *comforter*, and it means one called alongside who is capable of giving aid. It appears five times in the New Testament and is used only by John. In the Gospel according to John its four appearances have reference to the Holy Spirit as the Companion (14:16), Counsellor (14:26), Consoler (15:26) and Convictor (16:7), called alongsisde our Lord's own to take His place after His Ascension. The Holy Spirit would be, to Christ's own, all that Christ Himself was to them when He was here on earth.

The word *advocate* was used also in jurisprudence to denote a legal advisor who would plead as counsel for the defense. He would intercede in behalf of another. In a special sense the Righteous One is our Attorney. Jesus Christ, the only blameless example of human nature, continues to represent us before the Father, to plead our cause against the accuser (Revelation 12:10). In Romans 8 we are shown the double ministry of intercession in our behalf, that of the Paraclete who is in us (Romans 8:26) and that of the Paraclete who is with the Father (Romans 8:34). (See also Hebrews 7:25.) Our Advocate in Heaven pleads only that which is just. He asks for no leniency for sinning saints, no setting aside of the divine law. But as the "righteous" One who fulfilled the demands of the law by His life and substitutionary death on our behalf, He now represents us before the Father. His present work in our behalf continues as real as was His death in our behalf. The Righteous One having suffered for the unrighteous (1 Peter 3:18), the Father is now satisfied. We owe all to our blessed Substitute and Advocate, even our restoration to fellowship with the Father after we have sinned. We should rejoice in Him who faces the Father in all efficacy of His finished work and in the love and patience of His unfinished work. Hallelujah, what a Saviour!

The blessed provision for sin is explained further.

> *And He is the propitiation for our sins: and not for*
> *ours only, but also for the sins of the whole world.*
>
> 1 JOHN 2:2

The word translated *propitiation* is used in this Epistle
only, here and in chapter 4:10. The word is *hilasmos,* from
the verb *hilaskomai.* It suggests the idea of making atonement for, making satisfaction for sin. Our Lord on the
cross provided an atonement for the penalty of sin and a
satisfaction for the demands of a broken law. On this
ground, and on no other, can a holy and righteous God
bestow mercy on believing sinners, and remain just.

Under the old dispensation a ram was brought as the
sacrifice for sins, called "the ram of the atonement [propi-
tiation]" (Numbers 5:8). But on the cross Christ Himself
became the propitiation. He was "the Lamb of God which
taketh away the sin of the world" (John 1:29). By offering
Himself He was both the Propitiator and the Propitiation.
The Psalmist recognized this great truth, and therefore
knew that if there was to be any hope for him, God would
have to be and provide the Propitiation. He said, "If Thou,
LORD, shouldest mark iniquities, O Lord, who shall stand?
But there is forgiveness [propitiation] with Thee" (Psalm
130:3-4). I like to think that this very idea is included in
Abraham's words to Isaac, "God will provide Himself a
lamb" (Genesis 22:8). In the Person of His Son God offered Himself to be our Propitiation, for "God was in
Christ, reconciling the world unto Himself" (2 Corinthians
5:19). Thus do believers make up "the church of God,
which He hath purchased with His own blood" (Acts
20:28). The publican prayed, "God be merciful [be pro-
pitious] to me a sinner" (Luke 18:13). That prayer, prayed
by a million souls and more, has been answered at Calvary

in Christ's death. As the mercy seat covered the ark, even so the blood of Christ covers the believing sinner's sins.

There is a supplement appended in the words:

> . . . *and not for ours only, but also for the sins of the whole world.* 1 JOHN 2:2

Here is a solemn reminder for all Christians that God has no favorites, but that the Propitiation is sufficient for the whole world of mankind. This should serve as a constant reminder of our responsibility to take the gospel to those who are lost.

Also, there is suggested here the fact that God does not have one method for the sinner's redemption and another for the saint's recovery. Christ is all and in all. It is to Him the sinner must come for salvation, and through Him the saint must come for cleansing.

> *And ye know that He was manifested to take away our sins; and in Him is no sin.* 1 JOHN 3:5

The pronouns "ye" and "our" refer to the born ones, the children of God. It is true that Christ became incarnate to die for sinners, to provide an atonement, but it is equally true that He came to "save His people from their sins" (Matthew 1:21). "The point in the present passage (1 John 3:5) is not the mode in which Christ took away sins, but the fact that His having become incarnate in order to take them away shows that sin is incompatible with the divine relationship of being children of God. In other words, not the nature of the atonement is here in view, *but the effect of it in the life*" (W. E. Vine).

D. *The Penalty for Sin.*

> *If any man see his brother sin a sin which is not unto death, he shall ask, and he shall give him life for*

them that sin not unto death. There is a sin unto
death: I do not say that he shall pray for it.

1 JOHN 5:16

I have found this verse to be one of the most difficult to
interpret in the entire Epistle. But we must proceed pray-
erfully, for surely there is something here for us.

One important observation should be reiterated, namely,
the Epistle is addressed to the children of God. The words
"brother" and "pray" would substantiate that this verse
likewise fits into the category of the redeemed ones. We
may conclude, therefore, that for the child of God, "there
is a sin unto death," the reference being, of course, to physical death. This seems to indicate, not any one particular
kind of sin, but rather a state of sinning in which the
Christian continues. It most assuredly is not the unpar-
donable sin.

Here the brother who is in fellowship with God is exhorted to pray for his brother whose fellowship with God
has been severed because of sin. An erring brother should
motivate us to unselfish prayer that God will deliver him
from the error of his way, thereby prolonging his life. Do
not become a censorious critic, but pray for him.

To continue in sin is to "sin unto death," for sin tends
toward death. "When lust hath conceived, it bringeth forth
sin: and sin, when it is finished, bringeth forth death"
(James 1:15). In the case of the unbeliever it is both physical and eternal; in that of the believer it is physical only,
as in the case of Moses (Deuteronomy 32:48-52), Nadab and
Abihu (Leviticus 10:1-2), Korah (Numbers 16:31-34),
Achan (Joshua 7:16-26), Uzzah (2 Samuel 6:1-7), Ananias
and Sapphira (Acts 5:1-11), the moral delinquent in the
church at Corinth (1 Corinthians 5:1-5), and those who
partake of the Lord's Supper in an unworthy manner (1

Corinthians 11:27-30). Whenever God deals with one of His own in stern discipline, it has passed beyond the slightest comment from any of us. We can only leave the entire matter with our heavenly Father.

In concluding this study, I know of no more fitting verse than the following:

> *If we confess our sins, He is faithful and just to forgive us our sins, and to cleanse us from all unrighteousness.*   1 JOHN 1:9

The penalty of a premature death for sinning saints is happily provided for here. The branch need not be taken away, but it can yet bear fruit (John 15:2). Thanks to the grace and long-suffering of God we can confess our sins and know the blessing of forgiveness and cleansing. The confession is to God of course, not to a Roman Catholic priest, a Jewish rabbi, or a Protestant minister. Now I am not suggesting that it is never in order for a Christian to confess his sin to another of his fellow men. Certainly if I have wronged another I have an obligation to confess that wrong to the injured person. Moreover, in some instances it might be proper and necessary to make restitution.

The "we" in 1 John 1:9 means all of the born ones, including John. Confession of sin is not expected of the unsaved. The sinner is told merely to *believe* (John 5:24). The child of God is to *confess*.

The word *confess* is *homologeō*, from *hooms,* meaning "the same," and *lego,* meaning "to say." Thus "confess" means to say the same as another. Confession to God is the believer's recognition of each sin and the naming of it openly by speaking freely to God about it as did David (Psalm 32:5; 51:3). "He that covereth his sins shall not prosper: but whoso confesseth and forsaketh them shall have mercy" (Proverbs 28:13). The form of the verb "confess" speaks of continuous action. Confession is a continuous experience with the Christian. No child of God, who has any sense of sin's heinousness, could complete a day and go to sleep without confessing his sins to God. David said, "When I kept silence, my bones waxed old through my roaring all the day long" (Psalm 32:3). Wherever there is conviction of sin, the believer will hate it, confess it, and forsake it.

VI. TO PROCLAIM FORGIVENESS

1 John 2:12

A. Forgiveness is a Primary Blessing

B. Forgiveness is a Perfect Blessing

C. Forgiveness is a Personal Blessing

D. Forgiveness is a Priceless Blessing

E. Forgiveness is a Productive Blessing

I write unto you, little children, because your sins are forgiven you for His name's sake. 1 JOHN 2:12

Before we attempt a study of the subject of forgiveness in the Epistle, a distinction should be cited which exists between verses 12 and 13. The term *little children* appears in both verses, but a different Greek word is used in each case. Because both have been translated "little children," the meanings have been somewhat dimmed.

In verse 13 the whole family is divided into three stages of spiritual development, "fathers . . . young men . . . little children." The "little children" in verse 13 are either those who are young in the faith in relation to time, or else they are victims of arrested development. I dare say that some of you know exactly what I mean, and you know also in which part of the heavenly family you fit. The New Testament Epistles are full of the idea of progress. We are to "press toward the mark" (Philippians 3:14), "increase more and more" (1 Thessalonians 4:10), "go on unto perfection" (Hebrews 6:1), "add to your [our] faith" (2 Peter 1:5), "grow in grace, and in the knowledge of our Lord and Saviour Jesus Christ" (2 Peter 3:18). But, alas, too many remain "babes in Christ" (1 Corinthians 3:1). (See also Hebrews 5:11-14.)

It is to the entire family, regardless of the stage of spiritual development any one of them might be in, that God says, "Little children . . . your sins are forgiven you." Here in verse 12 He addresses the *teknia,* the *born ones,* and He tells them that they are in actual possession of forgiveness. In Ephesians forgiveness is listed as a present possession and one of the "spiritual blessings" (1:3). There God says, "We have . . . the forgiveness of sins" (1:7). The same fact is declared in Colossians 1:14. In each of these passages, including 1 John 2:12, forgiveness is a settled thing.

You are not a Christian at all unless your sins are forgiven. If you are in Christ, God's judgment has already been passed on your sins. The proclamation of the forgiveness of sins through faith in Christ is the good news of the gospel, for Jesus said "that repentance and remission of sins should be preached in His name among all nations, beginning at Jerusalem" (Luke 24:47). "Be it known unto you therefore, men and brethren, that through this man is preached unto you the forgiveness of sins" (Acts 13:38).

Now it is not enough that you believe in the idea of the forgiveness of sins. Millions recite the Apostles' Creed every week, and the creed includes the article, "I believe in . . . the forgiveness of sin." But the mere belief in the forgiveness of sin will not effect forgiveness and get you to Heaven. You need to experience forgiveness. If you merely read or recite the creed, and there is no knowledge of the fact of your sins and the guilt and penalty of them, then forgiveness to you will be never more than fiction, a mere notion.

I once read C. H. Spurgeon's great sermon which he entitled, "The First Note of My Song." He took as his text the one sentence, "Who forgiveth all thine iniquities" (Psalms 103:3). Now I seldom, if ever, copy someone else's outline. But this one is too good to pass up. You should have it! And inasmuch as it is now out of print, I am taking the liberty to pass it on. Keep in mind that forgiveness is one of God's spiritual blessings (Ephesians 1:3,7).

A. *Forgiveness is a Primary Blessing.*

In the famous Psalm 103 forgiveness is placed first in the catalog of blessings. It is primary. Please note that healing follows forgiveness. God will not heal the diseases of the soul until sin has first been pardoned and covered. In this text forgiveness leads the caravan and stands at the head of every mercy and blessing. When the believing sinner is reconciled to God, the first realized blessing is the cleansing from all sin. It shines brightest among the stars of divine grace and mercy. Every spiritual blessing is withheld until, first of all, the pardon of sin has been bestowed. An unforgiven sinner abides under the wrath and judgment of God and therefore he knows nothing of Heaven's blessings. We cannot expect God to deliver a man's life from destruction, or to crown him with loving-kindness and tender mercies, or to satisfy his mouth with good things while he is still unforgiven and dead in sins. Divine forgiveness is the path cut through the jungle of sin and its bitter fruits to the open fields of spiritual fruitfulness.

B. *Forgiveness is a Perfect Blessing.*

Our text says, "your sins are forgiven you" (1 John 2:12). The verb is in the perfect tense, which speaks of a past

completed action having present, permanent, and therefore, perfect results. Actually it should read, "your sins
have been forgiven you." Our Lord's first word from the
cross was a prayer. He prayed, "Father, forgive them; for
they know not what they do" (Luke 23:34). And then, before He yielded up His Spirit, He said, "It is finished"
(John 19:30). Here again the verb form is the perfect tense.
His prayer had been answered. A full and perfect pardon
was effected as the all-sufficient payment for sin. He put
away sin permanently and perfectly, so that all who come
unto God by Him are for all time forgiven. It is not that
they shall be forgiven at some future time, but that they are
forgiven fully and finally the moment they believe. So now
all believers can say, "We have . . . the forgiveness of sins"
(Ephesians 1:7; Colossians 1:14). Forgiveness signifies complete deliverance from the penalty of sin and the removal
of the cause of offence. Here is perfect pardon—"God for
Christ's sake hath forgiven you" (Ephesians 4:32). We shall
never be more perfectly forgiven than we are at this present moment. What a perfect blessing!

C. *Forgiveness is a Personal Blessing.*

The text continues, "your sins are forgiven *you* for *His
name's sake.*" Forgiveness is experienced by sinful persons
for the sake of the sinless Person. Everything that the Father
does for His Son's Name's sake is stamped with the full
approval of divine satisfaction. His Name includes all that
He is in His glorious Person, as well as all that He ac-
complished in His work. His Name is "Wonderful, Counsellor, The mighty God, The everlasting Father, The Prince
of Peace" (Isaiah 9:6). It is the Name "which is above
every name" (Philippians 2:9), and the only Name the
Father recognizes as the ground for forgiveness. The re-
pentant sinner who comes to God in that all-worthy Name

is forgiven for His Name's sake. "It seems most difficult for the mind to grasp the fact that, as revealed in God's Word, God does not deal with any sin in mercy or leniency. The sinner is never forgiven because God is bighearted. Any presentation of divine forgiveness which represents God as directly exercising clemency toward a sinner is a fatal detraction from the meaning of the cross of Christ, and a disastrous misrepresentation of the truth contained in the gospel. The forgiveness of God toward sinners, therefore, is a judicial pardon of a debtor in view of the fact that his debt has been fully paid by another, the Person of His Son, the Lord Jesus Christ." Thus it is a personal forgiveness, "for His name's sake." And it is precisely a personal matter for the one who is forgiven. Spurgeon's text says, "Who forgiveth all *thine* iniquities." John writes, "Little children . . . *your* sins are forgiven *you.*" That *He* should forgive *me* makes forgiveness a personal blessing.

D. *Forgiveness is a Priceless Blessing.*

Forgiveness is priceless because it is precious. It is a blessing which could not be purchased by wealth or works or weeping. When a man has done all that he can do, he is as far from forgiveness as the east is from the west. Though forgiveness is a priceless and precious blessing, it was nevertheless purchased "through His [Christ's] blood" (Ephesians 1:7; Colossians 1:14). "Forasmuch as ye know that ye were not redeemed with corruptible things, as silver and gold, from your vain conversation received by tradition from your fathers; But with the precious blood of Christ, as of a lamb without blemish and without spot" (1 Peter 1:18-19). And the purchase price was sufficient to pardon any amount of human sin. Have you ever tried to measure the greatness of the guilt of one single sin? Multiply the sins of one individual's lifetime by the total population of

the human race and you have an incalculable number of
sins. But blessed be God, He makes a clean sweep of sin!
When He forgives He forgives all of my sin forever. This
makes forgiveness a priceless and precious blessing. "Thou
hast forgiven the iniquity of Thy people, Thou hast covered all their sin. Selah" (Psalm 85:2).

E. *Forgiveness is a Productive Blessing.*

Forgiveness produces a happy heart. Jesus said to the
man sick of the palsy, "Son, be of good cheer; thy sins be
forgiven thee" (Matthew 9:2). The good cheer was not the
result of healing in his palsied limbs, but rather of the
forgiveness of his sins. The forgiveness of sins is a perennial
fount of joy. You see, when a man is fully pardoned, he is
changed from aversion and hatred toward God to a position
of love and trust. Before he was forgiven he was in the
position of a condemned man with the wrath of God abiding on Him. Now he is forgiven and therefore free from
condemnation, so that the fear of death and coming judgment has been taken away. There can be no greater joy in
this life than the assurance of sins forgiven. If any man on
earth has a right to be happy, surely that man does who
stands forgiven before God. The joy which is produced as
the result of the forgiveness of sins remains in times of
sickness and sorrow, pain and poverty. On the other hand,
such joy is not possible apart from the forgiveness of sins.
A man forgiven knows spiritual emancipation and fellowship with God, and in this experience there is joy at its
highest.

Thus far we have seen that judicial forgiveness has been
bestowed unconditionally upon the believing sinner. "Having forgiven you all trespasses" (Colossians 2:13), "ye are
complete in Him" (Colossians 2:10). But what about those
sins we commit now that we are God's children? This is our

problem as Christians. While it is blessedly true that our relationship with God can never be broken in view of the once-for-all judicial forgiveness bestowed on us by Him, we all know full well how our sins, as His children, hinder the mutual delight in our partnership with Him. This wrong condition of the Christian's heart must be dealt with. The sins of the saints must be forgiven and cleansed. Thus in 1 John 1:9 we have family forgiveness, the removal of the children's sins by their heavenly Father.

> *If we confess our sins, He is faithful and just to forgive us our sins, and to cleanse us from all unrighteousness.* 1 JOHN 1:9

God meets His children's honest confession with a twofold blessing. First, He forgives the confessed sin or sins. Then, He restores His forgiven child to his former position of uprightness and the joy of renewed fellowship.

There is no contradiction between 1 John 1:9 and 2:12. The latter verse teaches that initial act of judicial forgiveness which is necessary before the sinner can be justified and declared a child of God. This is the cleansing of *regeneration*. The former verse teaches the repeated acts of forgiveness necessary for the maintaining of harmony and happiness in the family. This is the cleansing of *sanctification*.

The word rendered *forgive* (Greek, *aphiemi*) means "to send away." The idea is taught clearly in Leviticus 16:7-22 where the live scapegoat is sent to an uninhabited wilderness bearing away the confessed sins of the children of Israel. The people were forgiven because the sacrifice was made and God was faithful. In 1 John 1:9 God is said to be "faithful." His faithfulness is essential to His being, and because of Christ's sacrifice, God's faithfulness is exercised toward His children when they confess their sins.

If our confession be personal and particular, offered sincerely from the heart to God, He will completely and graciously pardon and purify us. "He that covereth his sins shall not prosper: but whoso confesseth and forsaketh them shall have mercy" (Proverbs 28:13).

VII. TO PROTECT SAINTS

1 John 1:1,5,10
1 John 2:4,7,13,17,18,19,22,23,24,25,26
1 John 3:11
1 John 4:1,2,3,6,20
1 John 5:10

These things have I written unto you concerning them that seduce you. 1 JOHN 2:26

The word *seduce* (Greek, *planao*) means "to cause to wander" or "to lead astray." Phillips translates the verse, "It is true that I felt I had to write the above about men who would dearly love to lead you astray." The apostle is speaking here of false teachers who engaged themselves in the active effort of leading men away from the fellowship of the Christian Church. "These things" refer to the description and warnings about the antichrists in verses 18-25. Against all such the believer needs to be protected, and these verses are designed to do just that.

There are dangers that beset the Christian on every hand, but none more damagingly than those which come to us in disguise, "them that seduce you." They come, not as open enemies, but as professed friends. The history of man is a record of seduction. Subtle seduction caused the fall of our first parents (Genesis 3:1; 2 Corinthians 11:3). Christ warned His disciples that increased deception by false prophets would characterize the end of the age (Matthew

24:4,5,11,24). The Apostle Paul sounded a similar warning (2 Corinthians 11:13-15; Titus 1:10-11).

The Apostle Paul warned that the last days would be characterized by the successful activity of seducers. "Now the Spirit speaketh expressly, that in the latter times some shall depart from the faith, giving heed to seducing spirits, and doctrines of devils" (1 Timothy 4:1). The phrase "latter times" seems to envisage a time later than the writing of the Epistle. The departure from the faith here is not the final apostasy that will show itself after the Church is raptured, as found in 2 Thessalonians 2, but rather to those experiences of the Church leading up to that time. Paul warned of seducing spirits that would lead some from the faith.

In his Second Epistle to Timothy he wrote, "This know also, that in the last days perilous times shall come. . . . But evil men and seducers shall wax worse and worse, deceiving, and being deceived" (2 Timothy 3:1,13). Here the "last days" refers to those days that will bring to a close the Church dispensation, to be followed immediately by the Coming of Christ. In 1 Timothy 4:1 he is speaking of those days more closely related to the writing of that Epistle. In 2 Timothy 3:1 he has in mind that time near the end of the present age. However, in both passages, the warning is sounded against "seducing spirits" and "seducers."

This condition, in which seducers will lead men from the faith, will become progressively worse. In the latter of the two texts he says, "seducers shall wax worse and worse." Actually the seducers are evil "spirits," expert in the unholy alliance of leading men astray. They come to young people in the time of intellectual doubt, and they insinuate that the truth is false. These impious imposters have a way of deceiving. From the earliest days of the Church these divisive deceivers have been slowly, and often without observation, making deep and wide inroads into Christendom. These wicked men with their blasphemous denials are gathering strength for a final all-out attack which will precede the Coming of our Lord. They are doing much damage. In the sixteenth century John Calvin wrote in his exposition of 2 Timothy 3:13, speaking of these seducers, "They will succeed in injuring and corrupting others. One worthless person will always be more effectual in destroying than ten faithful teachers in building, though they labor with all their might." Like all manufacturers of munitions, the devil has improved his weapons with which to attack the minds of men. His emissaries shall wax worse and worse. This is progress of a wrong sort. Guy King called it "perverted progress" because their stock in trade is deception. They offer a gospel but it is a counterfeit gospel (Galatians 1:6-7), a perversion of the gospel of Christ. They appear as angels of light (2 Corinthians 11:13-15), when actually they are demons. They are "seducing spirits" with "doctrines of devils [demons]" (1 Timothy 4:1), and they work through "evil men" (2 Timothy 3:13).

> *Little children, it is the last time: and as ye have heard that antichrist shall come, even now are there many antichrists; whereby we know that it is the last time.*   1 JOHN 2:18

We know that we are in the final age of this present world. "It is the last time." What its duration will be no one can tell. The apostle had just finished telling them that "the world is passing away" (2:17), and now he follows up by adding it is the last time, called elsewhere "the last time" (1 Peter 1:5; Jude 18), "the last days" (2 Peter 3:3). The exact time of the consummation is nowhere revealed (Matthew 24:36), but we do know that our age will terminate with the Return of Jesus Christ.

The course of the age will be marked by the presence of "many antichrists"; the consummation of the age will be marked by the appearing of the person, "the antichrist." The many antichrists are the forerunners of the one outstanding evil personage, "that man of sin . . . the son of perdition" (2 Thessalonians 2:3). The word *antichrist* is used in the New Testament only by John (1 John 2:18,22; 4:3; 2 John 7). It may mean either *against Christ* or *instead of Christ*. Westcott suggests that the two meanings can be combined, and thus can mean "one who, assuming the guise of Christ, opposes Christ."

> *They went out from us, but they were not of us; for if they had been of us, they would no doubt have continued with us: but they went out, that they might be made manifest that they were not all of us.*
>
> 1 John 2:19

Those evil seducers were affiliated at one time with the Christian community, and were probably undistinguishable at first from the true believer. But time revealed that they never were partakers of the divine nature; they never really shared the life of God with the little children [born ones]. These were not backsliders since they never really were Christians. They were no doubt thought to be sheep when all the while they were like those of whom Peter wrote, "But it is happened unto them according to the true proverb, The dog is turned to his own vomit again; and the sow that was washed to her wallowing in the mire" (2 Peter 2:22). They gave proof by their apostasy that they never truly belonged to "us," the born ones of God. Their's was a doctrinal departure from the truth of the Person of our Lord Jesus Christ, a position to which they had given mere mental assent. Their doctrinal departure and denial of the deity of Christ proved that they never belonged to the Body of Christ. Their renunciation of Christ is the essential nature of antichrist (Jude 4).

Judas showed himself to be the forerunner of the many antichrists by his renunciation of Christ. He is referred to frequently as "Judas Iscariot, who also betrayed Him" (Matthew 10:4; 26:14-17,25,47-50; 27:3). (Read John 13:2, 21-31.) Judas, the antichrist, was a professor, and he "went out" (John 13:30), because he never truly was one of the "little children" to whom Jesus spoke in John 13:33. Our Lord never used the term "little children" when addressing His disciples, until after Judas went out. Likewise John uses it only of the born-again ones exclusive of those who "went out" (1 John 2:18-19).

> *Who is a liar but he that denieth that Jesus is the Christ? He is antichrist, that denieth the Father and the Son.*   1 JOHN 2:22

The definite article appears before the word *liar,* which makes it read, *"the* liar." The Antichrist, who will be the incarnation of Satan, impersonates all that is false, particularly in his open opposition to Christ. Our Lord said to the Pharisees, "Ye are of your father the devil, and the lusts of your father ye will do. He was a murderer from the beginning, and abode not in the truth, because there is no truth in him. When he speaketh a lie, he speaketh of his own: for he is a liar, and the father of it" (John 8:44). He is the one who habitually denies the essential deity and humanity of the Lord Jesus Christ, the fact that Mary's Son is very God. This is the claim of the Antichrist who, after the rapture of the Church, exalts himself above God and boasts that he is God. "Let no man deceive you by any means: for that day shall not come, except there come a falling away first, and that man of sin be revealed, the son of perdition; who opposeth and exalteth himself above all that is called God, or that is worshipped; so that he as God sitteth in the temple of God, shewing himself that he is God" (2 Thessalonians 2:3-4). Here the "man of sin" is the Antichrist, who will show himself to be against Christ and offer himself instead of Christ.

The words *lie* and *liar* appear in First John not less than eight times (1:6,10; 2:4,21,22,27; 4:20; 5:10). The word *liar* in the Greek is *pseustēs,* from which we get our English word *pseudo,* meaning false. Thus a falsehood is a lie. The ninth commandment forbids the children of Israel to bear false witness (Exodus 20:16). A lying tongue God hates (Proverbs 6:16-19). Christians are forbidden to lie (Colossians 3:9). "All liars shall have their part in the lake which burneth with fire and brimstone" (Revelation 21:8). These are solemn words taken from Holy Writ, and they would challenge us to go back and study those texts in our Epistle where prevaricators are dealt with.

> *Whosoever denieth the Son, the same hath not the Father: [but] he that acknowledgeth the Son hath the Father also.*   1 JOHN 2:23

This verse enlarges upon the statement at the end of verse 22, namely, "He is antichrist, that denieth the Father and the Son." Since no man has seen God, nor ever can see Him, save as He is declared, or made known through His only begotten Son, it necessarily follows that he who rejects the Son has likewise rejected the Father (John 1:18; 6:46). All who become confederates of the lie that denies Jesus Christ's eternal oneness with the Father, fall under the same condemnation as do the antichrists. Verse 23 teaches the essential unity between the Father and the Son, but more than this, it teaches that to deny the Son is to cut off oneself from the Father. It is not possible to deny the deity of Christ and acknowledge the fatherhood of God, since

the two acts are utterly incongruous. It is necessary that
one "acknowledge" [or confess] all that the Bible teaches
about the Lord Jesus Christ if he is to sustain a right relation to God as his Father. One shudders to think of the
fate of those first-century false teachers who rejected Christ
and His claims (John 5:18). And what about the present-
day pseudo-religionists who deny Christ? Surely their
greater light will mean their greater condemnation. He
who denies the Son is destitute of the Father, and is therefore a condemned man.

> *Let that therefore abide in you which ye have heard*
> *from the beginning. If that which ye have heard from*
> *the beginning shall remain in you, ye also shall con-*
> *tinue in the Son, and in the Father.*   1 JOHN 2:24

The apostle's appeal is now directed to the "little children" not to allow themselves to become sidetracked by the
false teachers. If the true doctrine relative to the Person of
the Lord Jesus Christ continues to abide [remain] in them,
that will indicate their relationship to both the Son and the
Father. This is what the false teachers did not do.

Twice in this one verse mention is made of "that which
ye have heard from the beginning." The Epistle opens on
this note (1:1), and it refers to that which they learned from
Christ and about Him at the beginning of His public ministry. The Epistle maintains this strong emphasis throughout (1:1; 2:7,13,24; 3:11). The Christian must be on his
guard against false teachings and false teachers. Deception
is to characterize the end of the age (Matthew 24:3-5,11,23-
24). Some of the deceivers will present their deception
under the guise of a new orthodoxy, but the very fact that
it is a departure from the Word, written or incarnate, labels
it as false. The first simple message which came from our
Lord, during His three years of teaching while on earth,

cannot be improved upon. Any attempt to tamper with that
which was received from Him at the beginning is a cunning
duplicity, a falsehood, a double-dealing. "Let that therefore
abide in you which ye have heard from the beginning."
God would tell us that in matters pertaining to divine revelation there is nothing new. Let that which you have heard
remain fixed and fresh in you.

> *Beloved, believe not every spirit, but try the spirits*
> *whether they are of God: because many false prophets*
> *are gone out into the world.*   1 JOHN 4:1

The end of the preceding chapter mentions the Holy
Spirit who abides in the believer. Here in chapter 4 we
are warned against seducing spirits. This warning is not
directed to a mere few who have to do with the oversight
of the assembly, but to all the born ones. Thus all believers
must know the spirits and be able to try [or prove] them.
The matter of "discerning of spirits" is a divine gift but
it must be cultivated (1 Corinthians 12:10). There are many
spirits—the human spirit (Romans 8:16; 1 Corinthians
14:32-33), the spirit of this world system (1 Corinthians
2:12), "the spirit that now worketh in the children of disobedience" (Ephesians 2:2), hence a test is necessary in
order to distinguish the Holy Spirit of God from the lying
spirits. All believers have the Holy Spirit. Through cul-
tivating an intimate knowledge and close fellowship with
Him, we are able at once to detect the counterfeit. "Quench
not the Spirit. . . . Prove all things. . . ." (1 Thessalonians
5:19,21). When we have heeded this first injunction, the
second will be much easier.

Precisely what is the test?

> *Hereby know ye the Spirit of God: Every spirit that*
> *confesseth that Jesus Christ is come in the flesh is of*

God: And every spirit that confesseth not that Jesus Christ is come in the flesh is not of God: and this is that spirit of antichrist, whereof ye have heard that it should come; and even now already is it in the world.

1 JOHN 4:2-3

The issue here is not the mere acknowledgment that Jesus Christ was a historical personage. The idea in these verses is not confined to the surface meaning in the Authorized Version, namely, "Jesus Christ is come in the flesh," but rather that "Jesus *is* Christ come in the flesh." The test is based upon one's conception of Jesus Christ, which is the fundamental test of every man's faith. "What think ye of Christ?" (Matthew 22:42) If a man believes and confesses the Incarnation, he is of God. This means he believes and confesses that Jesus is "Emmanuel, which being interpreted is, God with us" (Matthew 1:23), "that God was in Christ" (2 Corinthians 5:19), and that in Christ "God was manifest in the flesh" (1 Timothy 3:16). This is the true Christian's confession, and any denial of this truth is the spirit of antichrist. If it was necessary in John's day to try the spirits, it is more necessary today because seducers are waxing worse and worse.

. . . Hereby know we the spirit of truth, and the spirit of error.   1 JOHN 4:6

It is sad, but true, that among God's own there are heresies (Deuteronomy 13:1-3; 1 Corinthians 11:19). Never was there a greater need to be able to discern between Christ and antichrist, for in the final analysis, this is the real test of one's relationship with God (John 10:4-5,27-29). Believers need protection from "every wind of doctrine . . . and cunning craftiness," whereby seducers lie in wait to deceive us (Ephesians 4:14). The Holy Spirit and the Holy Scriptures make up that impregnable defense.

VIII. TO PROVIDE ASSURANCE

1 John 2:3,4,5,29
1 John 3:10,14,19,23,24
1 John 4:1-3,7,11,12,13,20,21
1 John 5:10,13

These things have I written unto you that believe
on the name of the Son of God; that ye may know that
ye have eternal life, and that ye may believe on the
name of the Son of God.   1 JOHN 5:13

We have seen that the Epistle contains a number of key
words and phrases which appear repeatedly throughout.
Some of these are *Father, fellowship, sin, little children,*
born, and *antichrist.* Another of these oft-repeated words
appears in our text. It is *know.*

About the year A.D. 70, there arose a sect which boasted
a superior knowledge over that of the Christian. They
called themselves "Gnostics," a term applied to anyone
who claimed esoteric insight and wisdom. Such a sect would
quite naturally gain many followers since there are always
the gullible who are quick to follow the man who claims
to know. Now, a man may claim to know something and be
correct in his claim. However, whenever anyone says he
knows there never was a universal flood, or that an iron
axhead could not have floated on water, or that no whale
or sea monster could have swallowed a man, or that Jesus
Christ is not the eternal Son of God, or that Christ could

not have ascended bodily into Heaven, you can put it down as an absolute and certain fact that he does not know.

The present-day Gnostic thrives in the realm of science (so-called). Science is knowledge gained from observed facts, so that the man who claims to know finally and fully about any given subject is boasting, in substance, that he has seen and heard all there is to know about that subject. The different departments of science, or knowledge, are divisible into (1) the *mathematical,* which treats of quantity; (2) the *physical,* which treats of matter and its properties; (3) the *biological,* which treats of life and its varied phenomena; (4) the *anthropological,* which treats of man; and (5) the *theological,* which deals with God.

In all of these branches of science, or knowledge, no man knows all that can be known. "And if any man think that he knoweth any thing, he knoweth nothing yet as he ought to know" (1 Corinthians 8:2). There is a theoretical knowledge which must be distinguished from the true and practical. When a man thinks he knows, but has a mere theoretical knowledge, he is inclined to become puffed up, vain, conceited, for such "knowledge puffeth up" (1 Corinthians 8:1). Too often we are more ignorant than we know, or will admit. He who boasts his knowledge is swelled up with pride. It is this self-satisfied man who feels his knowledge is complete, and he is often the first to want to impart instructions and the most reluctant to receive instruction. The Holy Spirit's use of the term "puffed up" in First Corinthians shows that Corinth had in it many Gnostics or scientists (so-called).

In the Gnostic society in the early days of the Church, there were two schools of thought that aimed their attacks at Christianity—the Cerinthian and the Docetist. Their discussions revolved about the Person of Christ, the former contending that Jesus was merely a man, while the latter, denying the reality of Christ's manhood, taught that He was some sort of phantom or ghost. The Holy Spirit answered these false claims of Gnosticism by giving in this Epistle some glorious and eternal facts which every child of God can possess with the assurance of intuitive knowledge. This divinely-given knowledge will prove, or confirm, one's faith in Jesus Christ and in the written Word of God.

The words, *know, knoweth, known,* and *knew,* in their combined appearances total not less than thirty-nine times in this Epistle. Indeed we have here an Epistle of knowledge, divinely given, therefore true, authentic, and final. No man can boast in this knowledge since he did not discover it through logic, by use of the spade, or in the laboratory. Such knowledge does not puff up. It tends, on the other hand, to humility and holy wonder.

The Gospel according to John was written that we might believe in Jesus Christ and be saved (20:31). The purpose of the Epistle is not merely that we might possess eternal life through believing, but that we may know that we possess it. The word *know* in chapter 5:13 is the Greek word *oida*. There is a difference between *ginosko* and *oida*. *Ginosko* suggests progress in knowledge; *oida* suggests fullness of knowledge, or to know perfectly, beyond the peradventure of a doubt. Saving faith in Jesus Christ gives the believer assurance that can never be destroyed. Some people say they believe, then they qualify their faith by adding "they hope" or "they suppose."

Seven times in chapter 5 we find the assuring words, "we know." The Christian possesses a knowing faith because Christianity is a religion of certainties. The child of God can be certain about his *past sins* (2 Timothy 1:12), his *present sufficiency* (Romans 8:28), and his *prospective security* (2 Corinthians 5:1). This is having a knowing faith, and it grows out of a saving faith. Without faith in Christ, we cannot possess His life. Without knowing that we have that life, we cannot enjoy and live it to the full. We need to know with a knowledge that is final and certain that we have eternal life.

Saving faith is not a barren, theoretical thing to which one has given assent in the past. Notice the form of the verb "believe." The text is not addressed to those who had believed something in past time, but rather "unto you that believe," who possess a present, active faith. It is the activity of faith that is the proof of life. And to this goal the Epistle is designed to bring the true believer. If your faith has been speculative and intellectual merely, and not experiential and practical, the Epistle has nothing to say to you. It is the child of God only who is to *know* that he has eternal life. If you have this life, you should know that you have it. This is the repeated and clear declaration of the Word of God (John 3:36; 5:24; 6:47).

That there are believers who do not have this certainty, there can be no doubt. The reasons why it is lacking are many and varied: ill health, nervous disorders, lack of plain teaching of the Bible, neglect of Bible reading and prayer, lack of fellowship with other believers. It is no virtue to be the victim of doubts and fears about the eternal destiny of one's soul. In our text (1 John 5:13), the stress is upon the experiential and intuitive knowledge that all believers possess eternal life. This verse has been called by some the key text of the entire Epistle, designed to enable the Christian to discern with assurance his eternal destiny. Have you or have you not been saved? The First Epistle of John will determine this vital question, thus we appeal to the Epistle itself. But remember, no unsaved person can qualify to know something about life while he himself is dead. Who would expect a deaf man to pass judgment upon sound? Who would expect a blind man to pass judgment on color? Who would expect a dumb man to respond to a lecture on the fine art of public speaking?

It will not be possible for us to study, in this one lesson, all those passages where the word "know," and its equivalent, appear. We have selected a few which obviously and convincingly bear upon our subject.

> *And hereby we do know that we know Him, if we keep His commandments. He that saith, I know Him, and keepeth not His commandments, is a liar, and the truth is not in him. But whoso keepeth His word, in him verily is the love of God perfected: hereby know we that we are in Him.* 1 JOHN 2:3-5

We are continuously in possession of the experiential knowledge that we have come to know Christ if we obey His will. Intellectual attainment proves nothing. We can prove that we know Christ only as we choose to obey Him. Mere lip service unsupported by this evidence makes one a liar (2:4). Loving obedience to the teaching of Christ gives assurance that one has more than mere theoretic and speculative knowledge. It proves that he has eternal life. To know Christ is to love Him, and to love Him is to keep His commandments (John 14:15). Only as we keep His Word can we know genuinely and practically that we are in Him (1 John 2:5,29).

> *We know that we have passed from death unto life, because we love the brethren. He that loveth not his brother abideth in death.* 1 JOHN 3:14

Love for the brethren is an infallible test of one's salvation, a distinguishing mark of a genuine conversion. Spiritual death is man's condition by nature (Romans 5:12-17; Ephesians 2:1,5); spiritual life is his new state in Christ (John 5:24). Hatred is common to the former; love char-

acterizes the latter (John 13:34-35; Romans 5:5). So long
as brotherly love is wanting, that is proof conclusive that
the one with hatred in his heart "abideth in death." He "is
a murderer" (compare 1 John 3:14 with Matthew 5:21).
(See also 1 John 3:10,23; 4:7,11,12,20,21.) This outstanding
characteristic of love pervades the whole Epistle. It should
be a surprising and shocking thing to see one Christian
acting in an unbrotherly way toward another believer
(Acts 7:26). Have we been transferred out of death into
life? Here is a simple test by which we may know (3:19).

> . . . *And hereby we know that He abideth in us, by the*
> *Spirit which He hath given us.*   1 JOHN 3:24

> *Hereby know we that we dwell in Him, and He in*
> *us, because He hath given us of His Spirit.*
> 1 JOHN 4:13

We will know that we have eternal life if the Holy Spirit
dwells in us, and we can know He dwells in us by the
mutual witness of our human spirit with Himself (Romans
8:16). If the Holy Spirit does not indwell a man, that man
is not saved (Romans 8:9). Christ promised that He would
send the Spirit to abide with us (John 14:16). The Apostle
Paul emphasizes the fact of the Spirit's indwelling (1 Corinthians 3:16; 6:19-20). But right here we are called upon to
make certain we have not been deceived by some other
spirit (1 John 4:1-3).

> *He that believeth on the Son of God hath the witness*
> *in himself. . . .*   1 JOHN 5:10

In 1865 Dr. James Morgan said, "Not only is it our duty
to seek this assurance but to cultivate it. It is liable to many
dangers and interruptions, and we need to cherish it carefully."

THE FIRST EPISTLE OF JOHN

Part Four

THE PERILS IN THE EPISTLE

IX. THE WAYS OF THE WORLD

One need not read far into our Epistle to learn that there are perils which beset the child of God. In earlier studies we saw something of the perils of sin and the antichrist. Our present study will take us into an examination of some of those passages which expose the perils of this world. The word "world" appears not less than twenty-three times in this little letter, and its frequent use suggests a threefold description of the world.

A.   *The World of Mankind.*

And He is the propitiation for our sins: and not for ours only, but also for the sins of the whole world.

1 John 2:2

This first use of the word *world* refers to the human race of mankind. This is the "world" that God so loved and for whom Christ died.

And we have seen and do testify that the Father sent the Son to be the Saviour of the world.

1 JOHN 4:14

Passages like the above refute the error of a limited atonement, that Christ died only for those whom He knew would believe on Him. Believers are exhorted to pray for all men, "For this is good and acceptable in the sight of God our Saviour; Who will have all men to be saved, and to come unto the knowledge of the truth" (1 Timothy 2:3-4). Only twice in his writings does John use the title "Saviour" (John 4:42; 1 John 4:14), and in each instance Christ is referred to as the Saviour of the world. In the first reference it was the Samaritan who confessed this great truth. The only limitations upon the atoning work of Christ are those imposed by man's unbelief and rejection of God's Son as his own personal Saviour. Let us never lose sight of the universal efficacy of the gospel of Christ. There is merit and sufficiency in the death of Jesus to meet the needs of every sinner. He died for the whole of mankind, from Adam to the last man. Christ died for the "ungodly" (Romans 5:6), for His "enemies" (Romans 5:10), for the "unjust" (1 Peter 3:18), for the whole "world" (John 1:29), "for all" (1 Timothy 2:6), "for every man" (Hebrews 2:9).

Mankind in itself does not necessarily constitute a peril inasmuch as Christians are a part of that world. It is this world that is the object of God's love, and for which Christ died. Neither race, color, nor ancestry exclude any man from being loved by God. Though all mankind is sin-laden and exposed to judgment, still God loves all. Christ at Calvary was the supreme demonstration of that love.

Though the Christian is still a part of this world of mankind as long as he is in the world, he is distinct and separate from it in the true and strict sense of the word. Any
failure to recognize this could constitute a peril.

The Christian's place in the world of mankind is expressed in the words of our Lord Himself. He said, "Ye are
the light of the world" (Matthew 5:14). As one witnesses
the apparent danger, darkness, and dereliction in the
world, the need for the light is equally apparent. We teach
our children to sing, "This little light of mine, I'm going
to let it shine." Really it is not a little light. It is a big
Light. It is Christ Himself. He said, "I am the light of the
world" (John 8:12). What a dark place this world is! How
sorely needed is the Light!

Christian, never complain that you are called to live in
such a dark and dangerous spot. All lighthouses are in dark
and dangerous places. That is where they are needed. What
do you think you are here for? ". . . In the midst of a
crooked and perverse nation, among whom ye shine as
lights in the world" (Philippians 2:15). Spiritually the
world is in darkness (2 Peter 1:9). Men need to be "turned
from darkness to light" (Acts 26:18). "Let your light so
shine before men, that they may see your good works, and
glorify your Father which is in heaven" (Matthew 5:16).

B.   *The World of Morals.*

*Love not the world, neither the things that are in
the world. If any man love the world, the love of the
Father is not in Him.*   1 JOHN 2:15

This second use of the word *world* means the present
order of human affairs, the world system. This world is a
member of the unholy trinity, namely, the world, the flesh,
and the devil. The Christian's peril is that world system

which is alienated from God and in opposition to God. Satan is its god (John 12:31; 2 Corinthians 4:4; Ephesians 6:12), and it is described as evil (Galatians 1:4).

> *And we know that we are of God, and the whole world lieth in wickedness.*   1 JOHN 5:19

The word *wickedness* should be translated "the wicked one" in contrast to the "Holy One" in chapter 2:20. But more of this when we take up our study of the devil. It is this spirit of Satan that denies that Jesus is the Christ. John says it is "in the world" (4:3-4). The subjects of this system are the hosts of unbelieving men and women, many of them religious, intellectual, refined, and cultured. The person who goes on loving this world system as a practice of life cannot love God. He is an unsaved person. "Ye adulterers and adulteresses, know ye not that the friendship of the world is enmity with God? whosoever therefore will be a friend of the world is the enemy of God" (James 4:4). In such a person the love of the Father does not exist, because the love of the world is incompatible with the love of the Father. Dr. J. H. A. Ebrard calls it the "extra-Christian world," the mass and multitude of the unregenerated, still untouched internally and experientially by Christ.

The Christian is exhorted to "be not conformed to this world" (Romans 12:2). More literally this should read, "Be not fashioned according to this world." To be fashioned according to the world is to have and look and act as does the unregenerated mass of mankind. The child of God has been divorced from the sentiments of the world's morals. He lives in this world, but he is not like it nor for it. His sphere of activity is in Christ.

My attitude toward this world system must be shaped by the Word of God, and the Word describes the world's attitude toward the children of God.

Behold, what manner of love the Father hath bestowed upon us, that we should be called the sons of God: therefore the world knoweth us not, because it knew Him not. 1 JOHN 3:1

Here we are told that "the world knoweth us not." The people of the world system, while recognizing us as Christians in name, cannot understand nor appreciate what manner of persons we are, therefore they cannot approve us. "The world approveth us not." And why does not the world approve us? The reason why is seen in the text as we study the word "therefore." The "therefore" has reference to what went before, namely, "that we should be called the sons of God." The men of this world do not understand the scriptural doctrine of the fatherhood of God and the sonship of His children. The average man in the pew has been taught to believe in the universal fatherhood of God, and this is so different from the true Christian's viewpoint according to the Bible. The world therefore disapproves us because we are, and are called, "the sons of God." When we say we are the children of God, the world charges us with being presumptuous, proud, and insulting.

Not only does this world system disapprove us, but it likewise hates us.

Marvel not, my brethren, if the world hate you.
1 JOHN 3:13

The verb *marvel* means to wonder at, to be astonished at. This is exactly how some Christians react when told that the world hates them. They are astonished at the fact that men of the world should hate the children of God. The Holy Spirit says, "Stop marveling."

Now I can imagine some of you are asking, "But why

should they hate us?" I believe we have the answer right here in the context.

Not as Cain, who was of that wicked one, and slew his brother. And wherefore slew he him? Because his own works were evil, and his brother's righteous.

1 JOHN 3:12

We all know from the historical account in Genesis that Cain was the bad boy of the family, while Abel was the good lad. But why would a nasty person hate, and even kill, a nice person? The answer is clear and plain, "because his own works were evil, and his brother's righteous." This is not a human answer based on a human standard of what is righteous and what is evil. It is God's answer and God's standard. "By faith Abel offered unto God a more excellent sacrifice than Cain, by which he obtained witness that he was righteous, God testifying of his gifts: and by it he being dead yet speaketh" (Hebrews 11:4). When the true righteousness of Abel, God's true child, showed up the unrighteousness of Cain, who was not God's child, then Cain hated Abel. This is the very reason why Judas hated Jesus. Jesus said this is why the world hated Him and will hate those who love Him (John 15:18-19). The Christian who identifies himself with Jesus Christ should not marvel if the world hates him. Our Lord stated it plainly in His high-priestly prayer, saying, "I have given them Thy word; and the world hath hated them, because they are not of the world, even as I am not of the world" (John 17:14).

Even so the men of this world are known by their identification with the anti-Christian system. Birds of a feather flock together.

They are of the world: therefore speak they of the world, and the world heareth them. 1 JOHN 4:5

Note the contrast—"ye are of God" (4:4), "they are of the world" (4:5). The Church of Jesus Christ and the world are two distinct and opposite communities. The false teachers who oppose Jesus Christ, like all men, had their origin in and of the world. The world is the source of their knowledge, thus they are limited to false doctrines and heresies. Having never been delivered from the world, they form their thoughts and habits and tastes in that direction. In plain words, they can do nothing other than exhibit such a character because they have never been born again. "Therefore speak they of the world, and the world heareth them." The world will not give us a hearing. It neither knows us nor understands our language. The language of Heaven, which is the language of the Bible, is foreign to the world, whether in private conversation or public administration. There are two men, two worlds, two languages, and two destinies. "The first man [Adam] is of the earth, earthy: the second man [Christ] is the Lord from heaven" (1 Corinthians 15:47). "For as in Adam all die, even so in Christ shall all be made alive" (1 Corinthians 15:22).

C. *The World of Materialism.*

The third use of the word *world* suggests the sum total of earthly things, called:

... *the things that are in the world.* ...   1 JOHN 2:15

... *this world's good.* ...   1 JOHN 3:17

The word *good* here is not used of moral goodness denoting uprightness or kindness of heart. It means material goods, things, riches, such as the "goods" [or things] the rich man accumulated (Luke 12:13-21). "The things that are in the world" in 1 John 2:15 are the sum total of temporal possessions possible to man. Here are seen the earth

and its temporal possessions in contrast with Heaven and
its eternal possessions.

Our Lord set the two in contrast when He said, "For
what is a man profited, if he shall gain the whole world,
and lose his own soul? or what shall a man give in ex-
change for his soul?" (Matthew 16:26) Now, it is not wrong
to possess this world's goods if one comes by them honestly
and considers them a sacred trust from God. But to all who
do possess them there is an obligation to assist the brother
who gives evidence of being in distress. The word *good*
(Greek, *bios*) is literally *life*, and here it suggests the means
of living, the resources for the maintenance of life.

These "things" are for the most part purchased with
money, the love of which is a "root of all evil" (1 Timothy
6:10). To love them and live for them is sinful. God has
promised to supply all our need (Philippians 4:19), therefore we should be content with such things as we have
(Hebrews 13:5). Paul learned this secret (Philippians 4:11),
and it will be worth our while to learn it too, for "godliness with contentment is great gain" (1 Timothy 6:6).

There is sufficient reason given why the children of God
should not cultivate a fondness for this world nor its possessions.

> *And the world passeth away, and the lust thereof:*
> *but he that doeth the will of God abideth for ever.*
>   1 JOHN 2:17

The verb is in the passive voice. All that is in this earth
is being caused to pass away. "But the day of the Lord will
come as a thief in the night; in the which the heavens shall
pass away with a great noise, and the elements shall melt
with fervent heat, the earth also and the works that are
therein shall be burned up. Seeing then that all these
things shall be dissolved, what manner of persons ought

ye to be in all holy conversation and godliness. Looking
for and hasting unto the coming of the day of God, wherein
the heavens being on fire shall be dissolved, and the elements shall melt with fervent heat?" (2 Peter 3:10-12) No
reasonable person would live for a world that is doomed to
perish. It is nothing short of mad passion that could cause
a man to live for the perishable. Sometime I would like to
prepare and preach a sermon on "The Three Worlds":
(1) The World that is Past (2 Peter 3:6), (2) The World
that is Present (2 Peter 3:7), (3) The World that is Prospective (2 Peter 3:13). Study Peter's three texts carefully, and
then decide which world you will live for. "Brethren, the
time is short . . . use this world, as not abusing it: for the
fashion of this world passeth away" (1 Corinthians 7:29,31).
This means that we are not to use temporal possessions
overmuch. They are transitory in character, having no con-
tinuity. "Set your affection on things above, not on things
on the earth" (Colossians 3:2).

Is yours a right kind of love or a wrong kind? Paul's swan
song closes on a sad note. He wrote, "For Demas hath for-
saken me, having loved this present world" (2 Timothy
4:10). Demas is mentioned three times in the New Testament. Once he is called Paul's "fellowlabourer" (Philemon
24). There was a day when he stood by Paul as a real
helper, but his love for the world made him a deserter to
the cause of Christ. His love shifted to the world and its
pleasures, but he learned too late that he made a wrong
choice. (See Hebrews 11:24-25.) I do not know with what
form the worldly spirit took hold of Demas, whether possessions or pleasure or popularity. I only know he became
a deserter to the world. Beware!

Thank God, none of His children need to yield to this
world, morally or materially.

> *For whatsoever is born of God overcometh the world: and this is the victory that overcometh the world, even our faith. Who is he that overcometh the world, but he that believeth that Jesus is the Son of God?*   1 JOHN 5:4-5

Our faith is in the mighty Victor who said, ". . . Be of good cheer; I have overcome the world" (John 16:33). The simple secret to overcoming the world is to be born again and to keep on believing. The victory is possible only to those who are "born of God," but not all who are born of God overcome the world. Some Christians have been overcome by the world. It is pitiful to see believers struggling to win a battle that has been fought and won decisively by the Lord Jesus Christ. "Thanks be to God, which giveth us the victory through our Lord Jesus Christ" (1 Corinthians 15:57).

X. THE WEAKNESS OF THE FLESH

1 John 2:16

A. The Desire to Have

B. The Desire to See

C. The Desire to Be

> *For all that is in the world, the lust of the flesh, and the lust of the eyes, and the pride of life, is not of the Father, but is of the world.*   1 JOHN 2:16

This verse is closely related to verse 15 and is an explanation of it. The world system is in control of unregenerated men who are, in turn, controlled by the devil. These men have one nature only, the old unregenerated, depraved nature of fallen Adam, called here "the flesh." Because of the corruption of the flesh, it stands opposed to the will of God and the laws of God.

The word "flesh" here does not mean the body, that is, the softer tissues of the body distinguished from the fluids, bones, and ligaments. It means the unregenerated state of man, the seat of sin in him (2 Peter 2:18). Paul wrote, "For when we were in the flesh, the motions of sins, which were by the law, did work in our members to bring forth fruit unto death" (Romans 7:5). This is another way of saying that when we were unregenerated, the desire was to do the very things that were forbidden by the law. But even though the unregenerated man might try to please God, he

92

could not. And why not? "Because the carnal mind is enmity against God: for it is not subject to the law of God,
neither indeed can be. So then they that are in the flesh
cannot please God" (Romans 8:7-8).

To be "in the flesh" (Romans 8:8) is to live "after the
flesh" (Romans 8:5), to be dominated by the corrupt nature
in man. On the other hand, to be "in the Spirit" [by the
Holy Spirit dwelling in you] (Romans 8:9), is to live "after
the Spirit" (Romans 8:5), to be led and instructed by the
Spirit.

The "flesh" and the "Spirit" are diametrically opposed
to each other, thus they have nothing in common. "For the
flesh lusteth against the Spirit, and the Spirit against the
flesh: and these are contrary the one to the other: so that ye
cannot do the things that ye would" (Galatians 5:17). What
man became in his nature through the Fall is, in the very
nature of the case, antagonistic toward God and impossible
of reconciliation with God. The flesh and the Spirit are
"contrary the one to the other," opposed to each other, set
over against each other in combat. They are opponents.

The flesh is infirmed, sickened, weakened, diseased by sin
(Romans 6:19). It is the dwelling place of no good thing
(Romans 7:18). The Christian should make no provision
for the flesh (Romans 13:14) nor put confidence in it
(Philippians 3:4) because he is under no obligation to it
(Romans 8:12). The weakness of the flesh is seen in its
threefold desire.

A. *The Desire to Have.*

John, in his Spirit-given description of this present world,
tells us it is characterized by *"the lust of the flesh."* The
world is dominated by the strong desires of the carnal nature of fallen man. The pull and propensity toward evil are
a part of every human being, and it is by means of the

body that these desires are expressed. "The lust of the flesh" signifies those inward temptations of which we all are too familiar. They are those irregular desires which, when committed actually, are usually done in secret. It is not merely the appetite of sense, which is God-given, but it is the appetite of sense deceived and dominated by the unregenerate nature. The appetite for marriage and its attendant privileges is not in itself the lust of the flesh, but in the natural man it may and does become the lust of the flesh. Indeed the flesh is weak.

B.   *The Desire to See.*

Secondly, the apostle speaks of *"the lust of the eyes."* This is the desire for indulgence which is prompted by seeing. It could be the lust for fine clothes, a new automobile, a modern house, power, or the lust to satisfy the sensual appetite for some base and immoral indulgence. It is prompted by the sense of sight and it grows in the imagination of the mind. When we see it, and our thoughts desire it, it falls into this category of "the lust of the eyes." Beware lest the eyes minister to the lust of the flesh. Jesus warns against looking on a woman to lust after her (Matthew 5:28). A proverb warns against looking upon the wine (Proverbs 23:31). We all must admit that there is a certain lust or desire that is satisfied by mere sight. It is a sinful lust and it often leads to the most degrading and sinful acts. The lust of the flesh stands for temptations from within, the lust of the eyes for temptations from without. We need to pray daily, "Turn away mine eyes from beholding vanity" (Psalm 119:37).

C.   *The Desire to Be.*

Thirdly, we have mentioned here *"the pride of life."* The word *pride* is *vainglory,* and it is used also in James 4:16

where it is translated "boastings." It is the empty display of, and haughty dependence upon, one's own achievements and resources. It is a man's boastfulness of his own way of living, a characteristic that will become more apparent in the last days (2 Timothy 3:1-2). It is that spirit which prides itself in wealth, talent, education, cleverness, and the like. This is dangerous. It grips men's hearts with such mastery that they will use any unlawful means to outmaneuver one another. This type of man is legion. He is a dead giveaway because he is a show-off. Watch him swagger! Hear him brag! He writes his own doom, because his dependence upon his achievements and accumulations makes him shamefully and sinfully independent of God's laws.

The story of the first temptation is most significant in this connection. "And when the woman saw that the tree was good for food, and that it was pleasant to the eyes, and a tree to be desired to make one wise, she took of the fruit thereof, and did eat, and gave also unto her husband with her; and he did eat" (Genesis 3:6). The three things listed by the Apostle John, namely, "the lust of the flesh, and the lust of the eyes, and the pride of life," are the three temptations with which Satan attacked Eve. These three carnal principles, in the words of the Apostle John, constitute "all that is in the world."

Satan stirred up in Eve the lust of the flesh "when the woman saw that the tree was good for food." Here is a purely physical appeal to the appetite. But the fruit was forbidden by God, and Eve knew it (Genesis 2:17). How subtle Satan was in his approach to her! She was deceived (1 Timothy 2:14). And how was she deceived? By Satan's distortion of the Word of God. The devil proposed a slight change by inserting the one word, "not." God had said to Eve, "Thou shalt surely die" (Genesis 2:17). The devil said to her, "Ye shall *not* surely die" (Genesis 3:4). When our Lord said that the devil "is a liar and the father of it" (John 8:44), He doubtless had in mind this incident, along with others. Any additions to, or subtractions from, the Word of God are bound to produce dangerous and deadly results, and one of these is "the lust of the flesh."

It is further stated that "the woman saw . . . that it was pleasant to the eyes" (Genesis 3:6). Again we see Satan's representative plan and master principle in action. None of us can deny that there is that in the world which is forbidden, yet is attractive to the eyes. Satan sees to that. Thus Achan *saw,* and *coveted,* and *took* (Joshua 7:21). The fact that it is attractive to the eyes conceals the danger that really lurks. Eve allowed her eyes to be fixed on the forbidden fruit when she should have fled from it, and the whole world was lost. David "saw a woman washing herself; and the woman was very beautiful to look upon" (2 Samuel 11:2). He continued to look and lust, and then he stooped as low as a man can stoop. But not all men look and lust. Joseph is a fine example of a man who, when tempted by the lust of the flesh and the lust of the eyes, fled from the temptation. "And the LORD was with Joseph" (Genesis 39).

The last of this threefold principle of evil is "the pride [vainglory] of life." Eve saw "a tree to be desired to make one wise." Read First Corinthians 1:18-31, and you will have no argument with what is written in 1 John 2:16, namely, the acquisition of worldly wisdom is the vainglory of life and is an evil pursuit. Martin Luther said that it is probably Satan's worst seduction to make man desire to know more than what God wants him to know. This devilish wisdom is deadly and clearly opposed to the wisdom of God revealed in the Scriptures. The appeal to the intellectual nature is the pride of life. This conceit of knowledge and intellectual superiority is a conspicuous and ever-growing evil in our day. It shows itself not only in materialistic and intellectual things, but in spiritual matters as well. Any preacher or singer knows how readily we show off our talent or our own personality. When we feel that we have it, we can hardly resist showing it. May God enable us to learn well the lesson that "the wisdom of this world is foolishness with God" (1 Corinthians 3:19), and that "this wisdom descendeth not from above, but is earthly, sensual, devilish" (James 3:15).

Yes, that is "all that is in the world, the lust of the flesh, and the lust of the eyes, and the pride of life." And it "is not of the Father, but is of the world." If we hope to escape being deceived by the devil, we will have to stand firm on the Word of God. Eve did not fall until after Satan had undermined her confidence in God's Word. Satan has nothing to offer apart from that which is "in the world," and the world offers nothing that will bless the believer and fit him for eternity.

Commenting on Genesis 3:6 and its relation to 1 John 2:16, Dr. H. C. Leupold writes, "Every part of the being of the first mother was drawn into the destructive vortex of the participation in sin. . . . The Satanic suggestion leads Eve to notice first something purely physical. . . . Then follows the statement: 'It was attractive to the eye.' The aesthetic finds itself appealed to. . . . To this is added intellectual perversion."

What we have been trying to say points up to the conclusion that the natural man is weak, thus he is easy prey to all that is in the world. Our weakness should serve as a warning to each of us who belongs to Christ. Christian, don't cast a longing eye in the direction of this world and what is in it. Beware of the lust of the flesh, the lust of the eyes, and the pride of life. "But every man is tempted, when he is drawn away of his own lust, and enticed. Then when lust hath conceived, it bringeth forth sin: and sin, when it is finished, bringeth forth death" (James 1:14-15).

XI. THE WILES OF THE WICKED ONE

A. *The Devil's Program*
   1 John 1:1
   1 John 2:13
   1 John 3:8,10,12
   1 John 4:4
   1 John 5:18,19

B. *The Devil's People*
   1 John 3:8,10

C. *The Devil's Prospects*
   1 John 2:13,14
   1 John 3:8,24
   1 John 4:4,6

When one has read the First Epistle of John he is confronted with the fact of a personal devil. In this small Epistle he is called the "devil" four times (3:8,10), "that wicked one" four times (2:13; 3:12; 5:18,19), and "he that is in the world" once (4:4). These nine references to Satan echo, in short, what is taught throughout the entire Bible. From Genesis through the book of the Revelation, he appears in various forms and is identified by various names. He is called "adversary" once, "Beelzebub" seven times, "Belial" seventeen times, "devil" forty-eight times, "dragon" twelve times, "Satan" fifty-one times, "serpent" twelve times. These, plus the many other references to him such as "the prince of this world," "the prince of the power of the air," "the god of this world," etc., add up to not less than one hundred seventy-nine references in the Bible to a personal devil. It is he of whom John writes in the five verses mentioned above in his First Epistle.

A. *The Devil's Program.*

> *He that committeth sin is of the devil; for the devil sinneth from the beginning. For this purpose the Son of God was manifested, that He might destroy the works of the devil.* 1 JOHN 3:8

In this one verse the "devil" is mentioned three times. That his program is an evil one there can be no mistake. When our text says, "the devil sinneth from the beginning," it does not mean that he was created by God an evil person to carry out an evil program, else God could be charged with being the Author of evil. The words "from the beginning" do not mean the date of the devil's original existence as a person, no more than the words "from the beginning" in 1 John 1:1 could refer to Jesus Christ in eternity past. The phrase "the devil sinneth from the beginning" takes us back to the beginning of sin, of course. Sin was exclusive of God's original creation and therefore external to the first man. Sin began with the rebellion of Lucifer, one of God's created angels, who became the devil (Isaiah 14:12-15). Sometime in the dateless period between the perfect creation of Genesis 1:1, and the catastrophic judgment of Genesis 1:2, Lucifer led a celestial revolt against God, and thereby became the devil. His original majestic and sinless career before the Fall is recorded in Ezekiel 28:12-19. "From the beginning" goes back then to the invasion of sin into the moral universe, that is, from the beginning of the devil's career as the devil.

The devil's program then is an evil one. He *"sinneth*

from the beginning." The tense of the verb here denotes that which began in the past and continues into the present. The devil sinned *in* the beginning of his career as the devil; he continued to sin *from* that beginning; and he still sins. When Paul traces back sin to the first man Adam (Romans 5:12,14), he is merely stating how we humans, who are Adam's posterity, became sinful. John goes all the way back to the spiritual origin of sin.

Satan's sinful program in the earth is described in Isaiah's vision in which he gives a panoramic view of the entire career of Satan. The prophet describes him as the one who "didst weaken the nations" (14:12), "that made the earth to tremble, that did shake kingdoms" (14:16), "that made the world as a wilderness, and destroyed the cities thereof" (14:17). All strife and wars, with their devastating aftermath, are attributed to Satan. This is pinpointed precisely in our Epistle.

> *Not as Cain, who was of that wicked one, and slew his brother. And wherefore slew he him? Because his own works were evil, and his brother's righteous.*
>
> 1 JOHN 3:12

The eighth verse recorded the beginning of the history of sin. Here we have the first recorded instance of hatred and murder. The murderer is said to be "of that wicked one." The wicked one is Satan, a designation evidently familiar to the believers in those early days of the Church. The words *"wicked one"* are the translation of *ponēros,* meaning active evil in opposition to that which is good. From it we have our English word *pernicious,* meaning destructful, harmful, injurious. A pernicious person is of the devil. To be "of that wicked one" does not mean that the devil created Cain, or any pernicious person, but that some persons have allowed Satan to control them so completely that they carry out his evil purposes for him.

The point I wish to make here, however, is that Satan's program is one of hatred and murder. He seeks to destroy men. Our Lord said, "He was a murderer from the beginning" (John 8:44), that is, from the beginning of his career as the devil. And the tragedy is that his moral likeness has been stamped upon the lives of too many men. God is a lover of men, while the devil is their hater. From the beginning of his career, the devil has been set on slaying man, both body and soul. We saw in an earlier chapter that "the whole world lieth in wickedness [or the wicked one]" (1 John 5:19). Luther said, "The world is a den of murderers, subject to the devil. If we desire to live on earth, we must be content to be guests in it, and to be housed in an inn where the host is a rascal, whose house has over the door this sign or shield, 'For Murder.'"

The devil is assisted in his program by a host of demons. It needs scarcely to be added that we are not to understand these evil spirits to have been created evil. Two passages in Holy Writ will furnish us with information we require to understand the appearance of this unholy host. "For . . . God spared not the angels that sinned, but cast them down to hell, and delivered them into chains of darkness, to be reserved unto judgment" (2 Peter 2:4). "And the angels which kept not their first estate, but left their own habitation. He hath reserved in everlasting chains under darkness unto the judgment of the great day" (Jude 6). Their first estate was one of holiness in contrast to their present state of sin into which they went wilfully. The devil continues to sin as he did in the beginning of his career as the devil, and so does the host of fallen angels.

B.   *The Devil's People.*

Two statements in our Epistle teach that the devil has
his own family and following.

> *He that committeth sin is of the devil. . . .*
>
> 1 JOHN 3:8

> *In this the children of God are manifest, and the
> children of the devil. . . .*   1 JOHN 3:10

The verb *committeth* in chapter 3:8 implies continued
action. It is *poieō,* a present tense participle, denoting one
who makes it his business to practice sin. His sinful propen-
sities and practices, issuing from his depraved nature, and
controlled by Satan, proves him to be "of the devil." His
actions proceed out of the devil as their source. The children of the devil are known by the fact that they "doeth
not righteousness."

In our Lord's parable of the sower, the seed, and the
soils, He said that an enemy came and sowed tares among
the wheat (Matthew 13:25). And then in His interpretation
of the parable, He added, "The tares are the children of the
wicked one; the enemy that sowed them is the devil" (Matthew 13:38-39). In language much stronger He told some
Jews, "Ye are of your father the devil, and the lusts of your
father ye will do" (John 8:44). The Apostle Paul said to
Elymas, "O full of all subtilty and all mischief, thou child
of the devil, thou enemy of all righteousness, wilt thou not
cease to pervert the right ways of the Lord?" (Acts 13:10)
Later when writing to believers about their preconverted
days, he said, "Wherein in time past ye walked according to
the course of this world, according to the prince of the
power of the air, the spirit that now worketh in the children of disobedience" (Ephesians 2:2); "For which things'

sake the wrath of God cometh on the children of disobedience" (Colossians 3:6).

Taking these passages into consideration, we cannot deny that Satan has his people, men and women under his influence, who indulge those evil passions prompted by him. Apart from a personal devil, it would be impossible to account for the multiplied efforts of wicked men and women to corrupt others. When men sin, and entice others to indulge in their unholy passions, they are but carrying out the purposes of him under whose control they are held sway.

Men are divided into two classes, the children of God and the children of the devil, and our text tells us that this distinction is "manifest." The children of the devil are known by virtue of the fact that they do the devil's bidding. And if they continue to remain under his dominion, they must of necessity share his doom. A tree is known by its fruit (Matthew 7:15-20). By our actions we bear the characteristic marks of our relationship. We are either the children of God or the children of the devil. The world is divided into two classes only, wheat and tares, the born ones of God and the born ones of Satan.

C. The Devil's Prospects.

Our Epistle does not take up the subject of Satan's final doom. This is dealt with fully by John in the Revelation. We will concern ourselves in the closing part of this brief study with what the Epistle has to say about Satan's prospects with the child of God. Four statements will show us that his prospects of overcoming the child of God are quite slim. The first of these bears witness to the fact that there were those believers in the early church who did overcome him.

> . . . *I write unto you, young men, because ye have*
> *overcome the wicked one. . . .*   1 JOHN 2:13

The "young men" had not yet reached the peak of Christian experience, nor were they just beginning. They were at neither the commencement nor the close of their Christian life. Shall we say they had reached the middle age of Christian experience. This is indeed a time when Satan attacks. Some of us know a bit about the perils of middle age. We have faced many temptations. Those to whom John wrote had faced the tempter and the temptations, but overcame them. These Christian warriors had met and mastered the adversary. They were "sober" and "vigilant" (1 Peter 5:8). But the real secret of their victory lay in their relation to the Word of God:

> . . . *I have written unto you, young men, because ye*
> *are strong, and the Word of God abideth in you, and*
> *ye have overcome the wicked one.*   1 JOHN 2:14

They had put on the whole armor of God (Ephesians 6:13-18), a part of that armor being "the sword of the Spirit, which is the Word of God." They had fought their fight to a finish, thus their victory was a permanent one. Their strength lay in their study of, and obedience to, the Word of God. In the Bible there is milk for babes (1 Peter 2:2) and strong meat for the more developed saints. The strength of soul that comes through the Word of God results in victory over the enemy. To possess divine truth is to possess divine strength. Men of the Word are poor prospects for the devil.

Another reason is stated why the devil's prospects are poor.

> . . . *For this purpose the Son of God was manifested,*
> *that He might destroy the works of the devil.*
>   1 JOHN 3:8

The effect of Christ's work on the cross was that He might break and nullify the works of the devil. If a man refuses to avail himself of the effects of Christ's work at Calvary, he continues in sin and must expect to pay its consequences. The work of Christ is more than a counterpart to the works of Satan. Our Lord's public ministry commenced with a mighty triumph over the devil (Matthew 4:1-11). It continued with repeated victories when Christ cast out demons from the bodies of men, women, and children. In all of these encounters Christ personally proved that He was superior to Satan. But it was through His death and resurrection that full and final victory was won against our adversary and accuser (Hebrews 2:14). (See also Colossians 2:13-15.) By the blood of His cross, Christ paid the full penalty for sin, making possible for sinners a way of escape from their archenemy.

Ye are of God, little children, and have overcome them: because greater is He that is in you, than he that is in the world. 1 JOHN 4:4

Satan's prospects against the believer are weak, not for any strength that we have in ourselves, but in the greatness and power of the One who indwells us. Here are two supernatural forces, each a person—"He that is in you" and "he that is in the world." Here are two Spirits—"the Spirit which He hath given us" (3:24) and "the spirit of error" (4:6). God, the Holy Spirit, is greater than Satan. Because the Victor abides in us, we can be victors over the evil forces about us. The battle has been fought and won, thus the ground and assurance of our victory lie in Christ's victory for us. He is strong, and we are "strengthened with might by His Spirit in the inner man" (Ephesians 3:16).

THE FIRST EPISTLE OF JOHN

PART FIVE

THE PRECEPT IN THE EPISTLE

XII. THE EXPLANATION OF THE PRECEPT IN THE SCRIPTURES

1 John 1:5
1 John 2:3,4,7,8
1 John 3:11,23
1 John 4:7,8,11,12,16,21

Reading through our little Epistle, I found the word "commandment" in the singular seven times, and the word "commandments" in the plural seven times. It was to me an interesting observation when I discovered that each time the singular was used it referred to the commandment to "love one another" (2:7,8; 3:23; 4:21).

The word *commandment* in Greek is *entolē,* meaning "a precept." Here it is an injunction, a charge to the "little children" to love one another. The phrase "love one another" appears five times in the Epistle (3:11,23; 4:7,11,12).

Among the several precepts in the Epistle, this one stands out because of its repetition.

> *Brethren, I write no new commandment unto you, but an old commandment which ye had from the beginning. The old commandment is the word which ye have heard from the beginning. Again, a new commandment I write unto you, which thing is true in Him and in you: because the darkness is past, and the true light now shineth.*   1 JOHN 2:7-8

In verses 3 and 4 the Holy Spirit speaks of "commandments." Here it is changed to the singular, "commandment." There is a reason for this. The subject of the precept is that of brotherly love. Christ said, "A new commandment I give unto you, That ye love one another; as I have loved you, that ye also love one another. By this shall all men know that ye are My disciples, if ye have love one to another" (John 13:34-35). One day a Pharisee asked our Lord, "Master, which is the great commandment in the law? Jesus said unto him, Thou shalt love the Lord thy God with all thy heart, and with all thy soul, and with all thy mind. This is the first and great commandment. And the second is like unto it, Thou shalt love thy neighbour as thyself. On these two commandments hang all the law and the prophets" (Matthew 22:36-40). And then our Lord added, "There is none other commandment greater than these" (Mark 12:31). "For he that loveth another hath fulfilled the law" (Romans 13:8). "For all the law is fulfilled in one word, even in this; Thou shalt love thy neighbour as thyself" (Galatians 5:14). "If ye fulfil the royal law according to the scripture, Thou shalt love thy neighbour as thyself, ye do well" (James 2:8). "Love worketh no ill to his neighbour: therefore love is the fulfilling of the law" (Romans 13:10). "Now the end [limit, goal, aim, purpose] of the commandment is charity [love] out of a pure heart, and of a good conscience, and of faith unfeigned" (1 Timothy 1:5). These passages teach us that the sum total of man's duty and moral obligation is expressed in one word —*love*. Love is the supreme thing.

"Brethren, I write no new commandment unto you. . . . Again, a new commandment I write unto you" (1 John 2:7,8). Here is a paradox, but a truth nevertheless. But how can this precept be both old and new? It is old in fact, but new in freshness; old in principle, but new in practice. The law of love is an old commandment (Leviticus 19:18), but the light of each new day, which brings the light of greater

knowledge, brings with it also a new unfolding of the lim-
itless and unfathomable depths of love. The word *new*
(Greek, *kainos*) signifies a freshness in contrast to that
which is known. The precept is old in time, but new to the
one who finds it for the first time. Love is not only old, but
ever fresh. In one sense it is an old commandment, rising
out of the oldest known laws of God to man. But it is also
a new commandment, restated and freshly revealed in Jesus
Christ.

If I look at my love for Christ from the point of view of
my first knowledge of Him, it is old, dating back to Decem-
ber 25, 1927. As I reflect upon Him now that I have come
to know Him in a fuller measure, my love for Him is new
and fresh. It is an old commandment dating back to the
beginning of our Christian faith. It is new in proportion
as we grow in grace and in the knowledge of our Lord
Jesus Christ. These are not two separate commandments,
but the one precept in its eternal and perennial freshness.

The precept is explained further in the definition of
love. Twice we read in the Epistle the words, "God is love"
(4:8,16). Don't miss the full significance of this statement.
It is not merely that God is loving, nor that love is merely
a quality which He possesses. Rather it predicates the very
nature of God Himself. He is the Author of all true affection, benevolence, kindness, and pity. Even as He is Spirit
(John 4:24) and Light (1 John 1:5), so He is Love. God, as
to His nature, is love, therefore it is His nature to be a
loving God. When we read that "love is of God" (4:7), it
is not merely that it is His property and thus emanates
from Him, as every good gift is from Him (James 1:17),
but rather it is the eternal principle of His nature.

The word "love" in its different forms is found fifty-one
times in the Epistle, more times than in any other New
Testament Book except the Gospel according to John. The

verb form (Greek, *agapaō*) and the noun form (Greek, *agapē*) make up the characteristic word of Christianity, and it is that word the Holy Spirit uses in our Epistle. It never was a common word in classical Greek literature. The pagan Greeks knew nothing of self-sacrificing love for an enemy. This love never has its basis in human personality, human passion, or human pleasurableness.

XIII. THE EXHIBITION OF THE PRECEPT IN THE SAVIOUR

1 John 3:16
1 John 4:10

Two words, "hereby" and "herein," introduce verses which exhibit the true picture of the kind of love contained in the precept.

> Hereby *perceive we the love of God, because He laid down His life for us: and we ought to lay down our lives for the brethren.* 1 JOHN 3:16

The word *perceive* means to know and understand. How can we know and understand the love of God, the love that God is? Only by experience. To perceive is to know by experience. No unsaved person can ever perceive the love of God. "Hereby perceive *we* [the born ones]. . . ." "He laid down His life for us." This He did in the Person of His Son, for "God was in Christ, reconciling the world unto Himself" (2 Corinthians 5:19). The love of God is perceived only by those who appropriate Christ's death for their own sins.

Have you noticed that we have here the second John 3:16? Both the Gospel 3:16 and the Epistle 3:16 are saying the same thing. At Calvary the love of God was exhibited in the sacrificial death of Christ. This is divine love in its greatest and highest expression. "He laid down His life for us." The phrase, "lay down," is peculiar to the writings

112

of John (John 10:17-18; 15:13). By this voluntary laying down of Christ's life the believer has come to know what true love is in its inmost nature. "Greater love hath no man than this, that a man lay down his life for his friends" (John 15:13). (See also Galatians 2:20.)

> Herein *is love, not that we loved God, but that He loved us, and sent His Son to be the propitiation for our sins.*   1 JOHN 4:10

This verse exhibits more vividly the love of God. Notice that there was no desire for reconciliation on the part of the sinner, no drawing nigh to God. Moreover there was nothing in the sinner to attract the love of God. It was "not that we loved God." "But God commendeth His love toward us, in that, while we were yet sinners, Christ died for us. . . . For if, when we were enemies, we were reconciled to God by the death of His Son, much more, being reconciled, we shall be saved by His life" (Romans 5:8,10). We were "sinners" and "enemies," still He loved us. That love which God is was exhibited perfectly when He gave Himself in the Person of His Son for "sinners" and "enemies" who hated Him. Jesus said, "If ye love them which love you, what reward have ye?" (Matthew 5:46) When God saw man's sin and hatred against Him, He did not turn away in wrath, but He was moved in compassion and pity, "and sent His Son to be the Propitiation for our sins." Never has the world seen so lofty an exhibition of love. "For we ourselves also were sometimes foolish, disobedient, deceived, serving divers lusts and pleasures, living in malice and envy, hateful, and hating one another. But after that the kindness and love of God our Saviour toward man appeared" (Titus 3:3-4). Twice the Lord Jesus said, "That ye love one another, *as I have loved you*" (John 13:34; 15:12). He perfectly exemplified and exhibited love.

In the Greek New Testament the definite article appears before the word "love," so that it reads, "Herein is *the* love." You see, it is not any kind of love, but that particular and unique love that God is. It is divine love.

XIV. THE EXPECTATION OF THE PRECEPT IN THE SAINTS

1 John 2:7
1 John 3:1,2,10,11,14,21,23
1 John 4:1,4,6,7,8
1 John 5:1

The precept in the Epistle is enjoined upon the children of God. Since God in His essential nature is love, and believers become partakers of His nature at the time of regeneration (2 Peter 1:4), it follows that "the love of God is shed abroad in our hearts by the Holy Ghost which is given unto us" (Romans 5:5). Thus the fivefold command to "love one another." Divine love is to be exhibited in the children of God even as it is exhibited in the Father. We are summoned first to behold this love.

Behold, what manner of love the Father hath bestowed upon us, that we should be called the sons of God: therefore the world knoweth us not, because it knew Him not. 1 JOHN 3:1

The Holy Spirit is calling upon believers to consider and contemplate this particular kind of love, this strange and foreign kind of love "the Father hath bestowed upon us." *Hath bestowed* is the perfect tense form of *didōmi,* which means "to give something," the gift becoming the permanent possession of the recipient. God's love to us is our permanent possession and we are the permanent ob-

jects of His love. The words *manner of* are the translation
of the one Greek word *potapēn,* which is sometimes rendered "strange" or "foreign." Indeed it is a strange and
foreign kind of love, a love from another world that earthly
kingdoms know nothing about, and which leaves the child
of God filled with admiration and astonishment.

With this new appreciation of the love bestowed upon
us, we are enjoined to love one another.

> *For this is the message that ye heard from the be-*
> *ginning, that we should love one another.*
>
> 1 JOHN 3:11

Those early Christians had heard this message from the
beginning of their first contacts with the Son of God (John
13:34,35), and as sons of God, love to their brethren would
be a manifestation of their new relationship (3:10,14). The
gospel not only saves men from the penalty of sin and
unites them to Christ, but it unites them in love to their
brothers in Christ. The evidence of one's faith in Christ is
seen in his expression of love toward those who are Christ's.
Whatever other precepts the Epistle unfolds, it enjoins
upon all Christians the precept to "love one another." The
duty of brotherly love occupies a large place in every believer's life.

> *And this is His commandment, that we should be-*
> *lieve on the name of His Son Jesus Christ, and love*
> *one another, as He gave us commandment.*
>
> 1 JOHN 3:23

Two things are stated here as constituting the "commandment," namely, to *believe* on Jesus Christ and *love*
one another. Right belief will result in right behavior. It is
useless for one to try to testify of his faith in Christ if he
has not love for Christ's own. The two are regarded here
as inseparable. Therefore it is useless to look for brotherly

love unless there be first faith in Jesus Christ. If this one precept to "love one another" were heeded, all trouble among believers would cease.

All true Christians are "members one of another" (Romans 12:5), and "are taught of God to love one another" (1 Thessalonians 4:9). This was one of the first lessons the early Christians were taught (John 13:34; 15:12,17), and it is repeated fifteen times in the New Testament. It was the plea of the Apostle John in his Second Epistle—"And now I beseech thee, lady, not as though I wrote a new commandment unto thee, but that which we had from the beginning, that we love one another" (2 John 5). If we love one another we will "not judge one another" (Romans 14:13), nor "bite and devour one another" (Galatians 5:15), nor "provoke one another" (Galatians 5:26), but rather "edify one another" (Romans 14:19), "receive one another" (Romans 15:7), "care one for another" (1 Corinthians 12:25), "serve one another" (Galatians 5:13), "bear one another's burdens" (Galatians 6:2), "be kind one to another, tenderhearted, forgiving one another" (Ephesians 4:32), "comfort one another" (1 Thessalonians 4:18) and "consider one another" (Hebrews 10:24).

> *Beloved, let us love one another: for love is of God; and every one that loveth is born of God, and knoweth God. He that loveth not knoweth not God; for God is love.*   1 JOHN 4:7-8

Five times this word "beloved" appears in our Epistle (2:7; 3:2,21; 4:1,7). [It is wrongly translated "brethren" in chapter 2:7.] It is used of Christ (Matthew 3:17) and of those who are Christ's (Romans 1:7) as the divinely-loved ones. This term is never applied to unbelievers. When we become the children of God, God has a special love for those who love His Son, our Lord Jesus Christ (John 14:21,23; 17:23). Someone may object and insist that all men are beloved of God. While it is true that all men are loved by God, it is equally true that none but the children of God are ever addressed as God's "beloved." Christ is the Father's beloved Son (Matthew 3:17), and if you wish to be accepted among the beloved of God, you must be made accepted in the Beloved (Ephesians 1:6). Just as any earthly parent has a special love for those children who are the fruit of his own loins, even so God loves with a special love those who are His children.

"Beloved, let us love one another: *for love is of God*" (4:7). "Ye are of God" (4:4), "We are of God" (4:6), and "Love is of God" (4:7), therefore love is the blessed bond of the family of God. To exhibit divine love is a proof of a constant increase in the knowledge of God, for "every one that loveth . . . knoweth God." To grow in the knowledge of our Lord and Saviour Jesus Christ (2 Peter 3:18) is to grow in love.

"He that loveth not knoweth not God." The one who is not habitually loving has never known God. Real knowledge of God has a practical effect that cannot go unnoticed. Love is therefore the test of life and knowledge, while the absence of love means the absence of spiritual life and knowledge. As we know Christ and love Him, we continue to love His people for His sake, for:

> *Every one that loveth Him that begat loveth him*
> *also that is begotten of Him.*   1 JOHN 5:1

Since every believer is a partaker of the divine nature, by which he is born of God, it is expected that his life will manifest love to those who are likewise born of God. Every believer who shares the gift of life in Christ will likewise share the gift of love to those who are in Christ. The person who loves God as his Father will also love God's children.

XV. THE EXPRESSION OF THE PRECEPT
IN THE SAINTS

1 John 1:6,8,10
1 John 2:4,6,9
1 John 3:15,16,17,18
1 John 4:11,19,20,21

But whoso hath this world's good, and seeth his brother have need, and shutteth up his bowels of compassion from him, how dwelleth the love of God in Him? My little children, let us not love in word, neither in tongue; but in deed and in truth.　　1 JOHN 3:17-18

The last phrase in verse 16 reads, "We ought to lay down our lives for the brethren." Notice that verb "ought." It appears two other times in this Epistle (2:6; 4:11). It denotes obligation, and can be made to read "owe." If we "ought" to do a thing, then we "owe it" to do that thing, we are bound to do it. The idea here is not that we could offer ourselves as an expiatory sacrifice for another. I do not believe that physical death only is meant here. The word *lives* here is *psuchē*, meaning "soul." This is the ego, the self-life. Read Mark 8:36-37, comparing Luke 9:25, where the words "soul" and "himself" are used interchangeably. Were we called upon to lay down our lives for our brethren, such a sacrifice could have no atoning value as had the death of Christ. But in the death of our Lord we have a standard for those who are His. Self must be crucified daily; the ego must be denied for the blessing and

119

benefit of our brothers and sisters in Christ. We have no right to say that the demand upon us is too great. Dr. Morgan wrote, "The apostles laid down their lives, and they did right. The martyrs laid down their lives, and they did right. Patriots have done it. Soldiers have done it. Men of letters have done it. And Christians should do it, too." I heartily agree to this, and I want to learn the lesson better.

We turn now to 1 John 3:17-18 where we have a practical illustration of one way of expressing our love for others. First, there will be a "need." Now there are plenty of needs around—needs of body, of mind, and of soul. For a professing Christian to have this world's *good* (Greek, *bios*), the necessities of life, and stand by watching a brother suffer from the lack of life's necessaries, how is it possible for the former to be truly in possession of the love of God? Here are two men, one possessing the means of living, while the other has need of those same means. The law says, "If there be among you a poor man of one of thy brethren within any of thy gates in thy land which the Lord thy God giveth thee, thou shalt not harden thine heart, nor shut thine hand from thy poor brother" (Deuteronomy 15:7). We all have had those occasions when our first impulse at the sight of need was to arise and give relief. Yet, too often we failed to render the assistance needed. If we remain in a selfish state, unwilling to help our brother in his continuing need, we disprove any possession of the life and love of God.

"My little children, let us not love in word, neither in tongue; but in deed and in truth." Love is in very deed a fine quality of the Christian's tongue. Kind and comforting words are not condemned in verse 18. We need to speak with soft and sympathetic words, but such words should be accompanied by helpful and heart-warming deeds. Too often marriages have been consummated as the result of

sweet words that seemed to come freely during courtship.
But in some marriages there never is that giving of oneself
to the other. You see, to express one's love in mere verbal
terms and not back it up with deeds, makes one a hypocrite.
May God save us from the hypocritical babble of loveless
insincerity that fails to demonstrate the compassion of
Christ.

Once more it is pointed out in the Epistle that apart
from a personal experience of God's love for us, there can
be no expression of that love through us.

> *We love Him, because He first loved us.*
> 1 JOHN 4:19

Concerning this verse, Wuest writes, "The word 'Him'
is not in the best Greek texts, and the word 'love' is not
indicative in mode but subjunctive, expressing an exhortation. The Greek has it, 'As for us, let us be loving, because
He Himself first loved us.' His love awakens within us an
answering love." The command to "love one another" is
not impossible of fulfillment on our part. The very fact
that He first loved us makes it possible for us to love. Do
not miss the point that is being made here in verse 19.
It is not that we love out of a sense of gratitude because
of His love for us, but rather that we are enabled to love
because He loved us. In other words, we love all of God's
dear people, not because their human personalities are
lovely and lovable, but simply because God's love dwells
in us. As the result of the love of God manifested to us,
we ourselves must also be loving.

> *If a man say, I love God, and hateth his brother, he
> is a liar: for he that loveth not his brother whom he
> hath seen, how can he love God whom he hath not
> seen?* 1 JOHN 4:20

Here the blow is aimed again at hollow professionalism. It is the case of one professing that which actually is not experiential in his life. At least six verses commence similarly, three using the phrase, "If we say" (1:6,8,10), and three opening with the words, "He that saith" (2:4,6,9). Love and hatred are incompatible; they are opposites. To say we love God while we hate another is to speak a lie (2:9; 3:15). There is no middle path. If you say you love God and really believe that you love Him, and you hate another, you are deceived. If you say you love God, and you know that you do not love Him, you are a hypocrite and a liar. Is your profession toward God a contradiction of your conduct toward others? In view of the incompatibility of love for God and hatred for men, it is to be feared that some professing Christians are being deluded.

Some years back I found it difficult to understand the words, "He that loveth not his brother whom he hath seen, how can he love God whom he hath not seen?" It was easier for me to love God, because all I ever knew about Him was good. But I could see the flaws and faults and unattractiveness in some of my brethren, and I found it harder to love them. Then one day God made it clear to me, from this verse, that if I do not love my brother, whose failures and unattractiveness I see, it proves the love of God is not in me. Actually the verse assumes the two to be an impossibility. The argument is confirmed by the added commandment:

> *And this commandment have we from Him, that he who loveth God love his brother also.*
>
> 1 JOHN 4:21

XVI. THE EXCELLENCY OF THE PRECEPT IN THE SAINTS

1 John 2:5
1 John 4:12,16,17,18

In your reading of the Epistle, did you observe the use of the words "perfect" and "perfected"? Each word appears twice, and all four usages have to do with the subject of love.

But whoso keepeth His word, in him verily is the love of God perfected: hereby know we that we are in Him.   1 JOHN 2:5

When any believer is keeping the word of God, the obedience is not the result of human strength nor of human quality inherent in man. It is the love that God is, reproduced in the life of the child of God who is yielded to the Father. It is the developing of God's love manifesting itself more and more in a practical way toward God and others. It is divine love reaching its desired goal in the child of God. Love is carried forth to perfection in obedience. This is the excellency of love.

No man hath seen God at any time. If we love one another, God dwelleth in us, and His love is perfected in us.   1 JOHN 4:12

Here again we are told that "His love is perfected in us" because "God dwelleth in us." The verse commences with the statement that "No man hath seen God at any time." This is the second time the Holy Spirit directed John to write this statement. (See John 1:18.) While it is impossible for anyone actually to see God, yet we may be sure of His presence in us if we "love one another." Moreover, our love for one another is a manifestation of His love being perfected in us. When God's love in us is having its full scope and sway, it is not necessary that a man see God, for then God is seen manifesting Himself through us. When the love of God in us makes us loving and selfless, then it is that His love is brought to its full and final goal. It is perfected.

> *Herein is our love made perfect, that we may have boldness in the day of judgment: because as He is, so are we in this world.*   1 JOHN 4:17

Love is not static. It is something that is ever growing. "And the Lord make you to increase and abound in love one toward another, and toward all men, even as we do toward you" (1 Thessalonians 3:12). Now how do we increase in love so that it might be brought to its full capacity of operation through the Holy Spirit? The text says, "Herein," and we ask, "Wherein?" The answer is in verse 16: "He that dwelleth in love." Thomas writes, "The reference to 'herein' seems to link the two verses (16 and 17), looking backward and forward." The cause of our love being perfected is our abiding in Him. The consequence looks forward to the day of judgment which we can face with "boldness." When God's love is perfected in us as shown by our love to others, we can face the Judgment Seat of Christ without reproach and without regret.

> *There is no fear in love; but perfect love casteth out fear: because fear hath torment. He that feareth is not made perfect in love.*   1 JOHN 4:18

We know that God's love is perfect, and when perfect love is in control of a man's life, fear is expelled. There is no possibility of the coexistence of perfect love and fear. The fear here is that slavish fear that brings with it torment. It is the fear of a guilty and condemned criminal waiting for the execution. The saint who maintains a Spirit-filled life will have no fear of being penalized when the rewards are distributed at the Judgment Seat of Christ. He will never need to view the future in terror or with the slightest apprehension. When love excels in a believer's life, it leaves nothing to be feared. Is loving service to God and others our choice and delight? Can we say with Paul, "The love of Christ constraineth us" (2 Corinthians 5:14)? If we can, then we may be certain that this is "Love Divine, all love excelling." God's love is perfect, to be sure; only let us make certain that His perfect love is being perfected in us. Let us seek the perfection of love as our Lord taught in Matthew 5:43-48.

THE FIRST EPISTLE OF JOHN

Part Six

THE PROSPECT IN THE EPISTLE

XVII. THE PERSON OF THE PROSPECT

1 John 1:2
1 John 2:28
1 John 3:1,2,3

We are left with a bright and blessed note on which to bring to a close these meditations in the First Epistle of John. Twice we read the statement, "He shall appear" (2:28; 3:2). There can be no mistake about its meaning. The fact of our Lord's Coming for His Church is in view. This is the Christian's prospect. In this concluding study of our brief series, we shall consider three verses and three selected truths which relate to the Return of Jesus Christ for His Church.

And now, little children, abide in Him; that, when He shall appear, we may have confidence, and not be ashamed before Him at His coming.   1 JOHN 2:28

Beloved, now are we the sons of God, and it doth not yet appear what we shall be: but we know that, when He shall appear, we shall be like Him; for we shall see Him as He is. And every man that hath this hope in Him purifieth himself, even as He is pure.

1 JOHN 3:2-3

"He shall appear . . . at His coming" (2:28). The word *appear* (Greek, *phaneroō*) means to be manifested, which actually is more than to appear. A person may appear falsely, that is, he may appear, and yet conceal what he

128

truly is, his real self. It is possible to see a person and yet not see him. To be manifested is to be revealed in one's true character. The two heavenly witnesses said to the disciples, *"This same Jesus,* which is taken up from you into heaven, shall so come in like manner as ye have seen Him go into heaven" (Acts 1:11). In other words, "We shall see Him *as He is"* (1 John 3:2).

We live in a world of make-believe. We are actors. It was the custom of Greek and Roman actors to wear large masks with mechanical devices to regulate the inflections and intonations of the voice. The Greek word for a play actor is *hupokritēs,* from which we derive the English word *hypocrite,* a pretender, one who appears in a false guise and thus does not disclose what he truly is. In Satan's world, where man has his earthly sojourn, men and women apply their make-up almost daily before presenting themselves on the stage of life. This superficial camouflage is applied both physically and morally. Recently (June 21, 1960) in a four page spread in *Look* magazine, there appeared an advertisement with the caption, "Skin-Deep Beauty: a $1 Billion Business." It went on to say, "Today, the face a girl wakes up with is rarely revealed in public." And most of us must admit that too frequently the heart we wake up with is rarely revealed in public.

Now it is possible that one might be judged wrongly by others. However, our job is to make certain that we are genuinely sincere, and thus we will appear before men as we appear in the sight of God. It seems that Paul was judged wrongly as to his motive for writing the First Epistle to the Corinthians. Then in the Second Epistle, he wrote, "Wherefore, though I wrote unto you, I did it not for his cause that had done the wrong, nor for his cause that suffered wrong, but that our care for you in the sight of God might appear unto you" (2 Corinthians 7:12). The apostle knew that the divinely-inspired Epistle he wrote, in which he rebuked sin and called for the excommunication from the assembly of the guilty offender, contained no personal bias nor wrong motives. Thus he wanted to appear to them as he actually was in the sight of God.

Are you guilty of play acting? Did you ever pretend that you were glad to see someone when in reality you were not? In this connection look at Colossians 3:4, "When Christ, who is our life, shall appear, then shall ye also appear with Him in glory." The verb *phaneroō* is used both times in this verse. When Christ comes with the saints to reign in glory, all the world will view Him in His eternal Deity and Godhead. Elsewhere John wrote, "Behold, He cometh with clouds; and every eye shall see Him" (Revelation 1:7). Not only will He be manifested, but we also will be manifested with Him. Paul wrote, "Your life is hid with Christ in God" (Colossians 3:3). In that day we will no more be hid, that is, the life in Christ, which is now concealed from the unsaved, will be manifested then. John wrote, "The world knoweth us not" (1 John 3:1). But God has a plan for our manifestation, namely, "That in the ages to come He might shew the exceeding riches of His grace in His kindness toward us through Christ Jesus" (Ephesians 2:7). When our Lord comes in that great day to be manifested to the world, our relation to Him will also be a manifest one.

We are assured that Christ will appear. The text reads, "When He shall appear." Christ has "appeared to put away sin by the sacrifice of Himself" (Hebrews 9:26), He does "now appear in the presence of God for us" (Hebrews 9:24), and "He shall appear the second time" (Hebrews 9:28). The word *phaneroō* [to manifest] is used in reference to our Lord's Incarnation (1 Timothy 3:16; 1 John

1:2), His appearance after His resurrection to His disciples (John 21:1,4), and His Coming again (Colossians 3:4).

The Person of the Prospect is emphasized still further in the use of the words "His coming" (2:28). The word *coming* (Greek, *parousia*) literally means "presence." *Parousia* is made up of *para,* meaning "beside," and the participial form of the verb *to be,* thus the compound word gives to us the literal meaning, "being beside." In classical Greek it was used in reference to the presence of a person. Where it is used prophetically in the New Testament, it refers to the real Presence of Christ when He descends again from Heaven. The Parousia of Jesus Christ is a defined period with a commencement (1 Thessalonians 4:15; 5:23; 2 Thessalonians 2:1); a course (Matthew 24:3,37,39); and a conclusion (Matthew 24:27; 2 Thessalonians 2:8).

Yes, "He shall appear . . . at His coming . . . and every eye shall see Him." This sublime event will be public. At some time and in some phase of His judicial administration Christ shall be manifested to every one who has lived and to every one who shall live. So universal will be the manifestation of the Son of God that nothing will be hid from Him. His appearing will be as visible as the lightning, "For as the lightning cometh out of the east, and shineth even unto the west; so shall also the coming of the Son of man be" (Matthew 24:27). The Roman soldiers who inflicted the wounds upon His body shall see Him, for the Scripture says, "And they shall look upon Me whom they have pierced" (Zechariah 12:10). He will not be the object of admiration to those who hated Him. They "shall wail because of Him" (Revelation 1:7), and at the very sight of this august and omnipotent One, they shall call upon the rocks and the mountains to fall on them and to hide them from His face (Revelation 6:16). "And in those days shall men seek death, and shall not find it; and shall desire to die, and death shall flee from them" (Revelation 9:6). When all mankind beholds that awful splendor of the Holy One, terror will seize every heart. "And then shall all the tribes of the earth mourn, and they shall see the Son of man coming in the clouds of heaven with power and great glory" (Matthew 24:30). The prophet Zechariah describes Christ's appearing before those who rejected Him as a time of "bitterness" for them (Zechariah 12:10). For the unbeliever, "That day is a day of wrath, a day of trouble and distress, a day of wasteness and desolation, a day of darkness and gloominess, a day of clouds and thick darkness" (Zephaniah 1:15). I do not wonder that the unsaved have no appreciation whatever for the Christian doctrine of the Second Coming of Jesus Christ. Nevertheless He shall appear.

XVIII. THE PREPARATION FOR THE PROSPECT

1 John 2:6,9,10,14,17,19,24,27,28
1 John 3:2,3,6,9,14,15,24
1 John 4:12,13,15,16

"And now, little children, abide in Him. . . ." In view of Christ's appearing first for His Church, believers are exhorted to "abide in Him." Because of the uncertainty of the time of His Coming we should "be constantly abiding in Him." This is the force of the verb *abide*, and the appeal cannot be urged upon us too often.

The verb *abide* (Greek, *menō*) is found in our Epistle not less than twenty-two times. It is translated *abide* twelve times (2:6,10,14,17,24,27,28; 3:6,14,15,24); *continue* two times (2:19,24); *remain* two times (2:24; 3:9) and *dwell* six times (3:24; 4:12,13,15,16). Thus we see that the meaning of the word *abide* is to continue, remain, dwell.

Three times in the Epistle God is said to abide in the believer. "And hereby we know that He abideth in us, by the Spirit which He hath given us" (3:24). From other passages, as well as from personal experience, we know that the born-again one is the dwelling place, the abiding place of the Holy Spirit (John 14:16; 1 Corinthians 3:16). "God dwelleth in us" (1 John 4:12). The possession of the Holy Spirit is the evidence of the new life in the believer and of the fact that God is abiding in him. We may know, and we ought to know—and if we have been born again

we do know—that God abides in us. The way by which
such knowledge is attained is through a person-to-person
communication. "The Spirit [Holy Spirit] . . . beareth
witness with our spirit, that we are the children of God"
(Romans 8:16). There can be no doubt about the Lord
abiding in us. The fact of it is stated positively in the
Epistle.

But our text does exhort the Christian to abide in Him.
"And now, little children, abide in Him" (2:28). Here we
are simply being told to remain in fellowship with Him,
to continue in unbroken communion with Him, to dwell
in right relation with Him. In Him life both commences
and continues. The fruitful life is the abiding life (John
15:4-5). The prayer life is the abiding life (John 15:7). The
moment we allow any sin to cut us off from that sweet and
blessed fellowship with our Lord, then it is that our lives
become fruitless and prayer is ineffective. Jesus said, "Without Me ye can do nothing" (John 15:5).

Now, we know that Christ is going to appear to gather
His own unto Himself. But how do you think any one of
us might feel if he or she is not abiding in Christ when He
comes for us? Our verse gives to us the true answer. "Abide
in Him; that, when He shall appear, we may have confidence." Grace put us in touch with Christ, but if we refuse
to stay where grace has put us, we will not have "confidence" when He comes. The word *confidence* (Greek,
parrhēsia) is translated *boldness* in the Revised Version,
and means literally "boldness of speech." You see, immediately following His appearance for us, "we must all appear before the judgment seat of Christ; that every one
may receive the things done in his body, according to that
he hath done, whether it be good or bad" (2 Corinthians
5:10). Here again we have the word *appear* (Greek, *phaneroō*), which means to be manifested in one's true character.

When our Lord appears "as He is," then we will be exposed as we are. If we have failed to abide in Christ, that is, if we are out of fellowship when He appears and thus not on speaking terms with Him, you can see how there will be no freedom of speech when we see Him face to face.

I like to think of Enoch in this connection. When Enoch was caught up alive to Heaven, he was walking with God; he was in fellowship with God; he was communing with God. Then, suddenly he disappeared. The Scripture says, "And Enoch walked with God: and he was not; for God took him" (Genesis 5:24). Enoch was not ashamed when the Lord came for him. There was no embarrassing silence at that moment for him. There was no need for any sort of an adjustment to that meeting with the Lord. He had been walking with God and was ready. There was holy boldness and an instantaneous freedom of speech. Every Christian knows something of the sweetness of those intimate moments before the throne of grace, when we stand before God boldly (Hebrews 4:16), speaking to Him freely. Surely it is just such an experience we would covet for ourselves at His appearing. To abide in Him, then, is the finest preparation in view of the prospect of His Coming.

Further preparation for our Lord's appearing is found in 1 John 3:2-3. After the statement, "He shall appear," there follows in verse 3 the words, "And every man that hath this hope in Him purifieth himself, even as He is pure." Here our Lord's Return is called the Christian's "hope," and there is attached to it a moral purity. This hope should ever stir us to put all uncleanness out of our lives. The hope of seeing Him "as He is" (3:2) should arouse in us a desire and determination to be "as He is" (3:3). Indeed the hope of Christ's Return is a purifying hope, urging us to be cleansed from every defilement and inconsistency, and to resist every evil influence. Every Christian I have ever known, who believed in the Lord's Return and who gave serious thought to His Coming, also made serious preparation for it. Paul's exhortation on the blessed hope emphasizes this matter of purity (Titus 2:11-14). Peter likewise linked Christ's Second Coming with a challenge to moral cleanliness (2 Peter 3:10-14). This blessed hope is an incentive to patience (James 5:7-8), sincerity (Philippians 1:10), charitableness (1 Corinthians 4:5), and considerateness (Philippians 4:5, Amplified). Nothing could possibly have a more sanctifying effect on the behavior of a child of God than the thought of the imminent Return of our Lord Jesus Christ. Heart occupation with the Saviour's Return is a strong force in weaning Christians away from the world. "Watch therefore: for ye know not what hour your Lord doth come. . . . Therefore be ye also ready: for in such an hour as ye think not the Son of man cometh" (Matthew 24:42,44).

Look at the word "hope" for a moment. Hope always concerns the future. We never hope for something that has taken place in the past. Moreover, hope relates only to that which we know will be for our good and to that which we know is possible. The Christian's hope in the New Testament is a living hope which has as its foundation the historical fact of the Resurrection of Jesus Christ (1 Peter 1:3). Guy H. King said of hope: "In the New Testament it always means a certainty. It is not, 'I have not got it, but I hope I may,' but 'I have not yet got it, but I know I shall.' " It is certain. To know for certain that my Lord is coming will cause me to prepare for that prospect.

One word more about our "hope." Beware lest you misconstrue the words "in Him" in 1 John 3:3. The little word *in* is more accurately rendered "upon." It is not that the hope of the Christian is in himself or within himself. In no sense of the word does the hope rest upon ourselves.

The real meaning of verse 3 is, "And every man that hath this hope set upon Him [Christ]." Are you asking what the major difference might be? The difference is a big one and I'll tell you exactly what it is: the wrong interpretation causes you to look at yourself; the right interpretation keeps your eyes on Christ.

XIX. THE POTENTIAL IN THE PROSPECT

1 John 3:2

First, "we shall be like Him" (1 John 3:2). This means we shall have a body like His. Paul wrote about this great potential. He said, "For our conversation is in heaven; from whence also we look for the Saviour, the Lord Jesus Christ: Who shall change our vile body, that it may be fashioned like unto His glorious body, according to the working whereby He is able even to subdue all things unto Himself" (Philippians 3:20-21). The word *vile* (Greek, *tapeinōsis*) is rendered "humiliation." Man's present body is a humiliated body, humiliated by sin, sickness, and death. The most powerful and robust bodies are eventually brought low with the passing of time. But when Christ appears for His own, our bodies will be fashioned like unto His. "Behold, I shew you a mystery; We shall not all sleep, but we shall all be changed, In a moment, in the twinkling of an eye, at the last trump: for the trumpet shall sound, and the dead shall be raised incorruptible, and we shall be changed" (1 Corinthians 15:51-52). Twice here the Holy Spirit reminds us that "we shall be changed."

God's great plan of salvation for man is complete and perfect. It provides for the sinner's *justification,* that act of God whereby He declares righteous the believing sinner, having Himself removed the guilt and penalty of sin by laying it on His Son at Calvary, and bestowing a perfect and positive righteousness in which the believing one

138

stands uncondemned in Jesus Christ. It provides for the believer's *sanctification,* that act of God whereby He breaks the power of sin in His children, making it possible for them to be victorious over sin by means of His own nature dwelling in them in the Person of the Holy Spirit. It provides for the Christian's *glorification,* that act of God whereby He transforms the humiliated body into a glorified body, adapting it to its eternal abode. "For whom He did foreknow, He also did predestinate to be conformed to the image of His Son, that He might be the firstborn among many brethren. Moreover whom He did predestinate, them He also called: and whom He called, them He also justified: and whom He justified, them He also glorified" (Romans 8:29-30). It is the final act of glorification for which the believer waits, referred to in the Bible as "the redemption of our body" (Romans 8:23). Our humiliated body will be conformed, as to its outward expression, to the body of Christ's glory. Thus, declares our text in First John, "we shall be like Him."

The Bible describes this body. "So also is the resurrection of the dead. It is sown in corruption; it is raised in incorruption" (1 Corinthians 15:42). Keep in mind that the contrast here is between two living bodies, not between a dead body and a living one. While it is true that the dead body in the grave is characterized by corruption, this is so only because this is the characteristic operating in the body while it lives. Corruption is characteristic of my body now, even at its best. Corruption is liable to disease, death, and decay. Such a body will not do for a resurrection body since the resurrection body must be adapted to eternity. The body of our risen Lord will never know sickness, pain, old age, or death. "We shall be like Him." This is the glorious potential in the prospect of His appearing.

The resurrection body is described further with the

words, "It is sown in dishonour; it is raised in glory" (1 Corinthians 15:43). It necessarily follows that that which is corrupt is dishonorable. The corruptible body has in it that quality of vileness, humiliation, and shame. The most glowing display of feminine loveliness or masculine vigor is devoid of the imperishable element, thus if you insist upon attaching honor to your body, it is a perishable and perishing honor, and that is no honor at all. But, thank God, the new body will be a body of glory, glorious and glorified. "We shall be like Him." This is the potential in the prospect of His appearing.

Of the resurrection body the Scripture adds, "It is sown in weakness; it is raised in power" (1 Corinthians 15:43). How impotent is the strongest human body against the forces of nature! Caught in a swift ocean current or a whirling tornado, trapped in a collapsed mine, struck by a bolt of lightning, the body lies weak and often lifeless. But the resurrection body will never be subject to weariness and weakness. It shall never become tired, never need rest nor replenishing. God will see to that. He will give to us a body suited to endless existence, a body like that of our blessed Lord. "We shall be like Him." This is the potential in the prospect of His appearing.

Finally, "It is sown a natural body; it is raised a spiritual body. There is a natural body, and there is a spiritual body" (1 Corinthians 15:44). The natural body is characterized by corruptibility, dishonor, and weakness, and it is fitted for life on this earth. But God has fitted His children for a higher life, and therefore He will give to them a body that will not be subject to the laws of nature as our bodies are today. This present body, being a natural or soulish body, is not always subject to the spirit. "The spirit indeed is willing, but the flesh is weak" (Matthew 26:41). But in my resurrection body there will be nothing to hinder me from living in the spirit world, nor can any power in that day hinder my new body from yielding fully to the mind of the Spirit.

One of the outstanding marvels of the appearance of Christ is that we, in a moment, shall be changed into His perfect likeness. There are many things about the future we do not know. But there are two things of which we are certain—"He shall appear" and "we shall be like Him." This is the consummation of our redemption. The old man will be done with forever and we will be transformed into the perfect image and likeness of Him who created and redeemed us. What is now a process (2 Corinthians 3:18) will be instantaneously perfected when we see Jesus. This is the potential in the prospect of His appearing.

THE SECOND EPISTLE
OF
JOHN

XX. THE SECOND EPISTLE OF JOHN

There is a note of similarity in these three Epistles attributed to the pen of the Apostle John. I find no problem in accepting the fact that John wrote all three. The reader will find peculiar forms common to all. The Second and Third Epistles are small yet very important parts of the New Testament, brevity being no sign of unimportance. This precious little letter, while the shortest book in the New Testament, may well engage the thoughts of us all since there are lessons to be learned that we cannot afford to slight.

While there is similarity between the First and Second Epistles of John, there is likewise individuality. The first is a general letter addressed to Christians at large; the second is directed to an individual. The second might be unoriginal to a large extent, yet there are two distinctive verses peculiar to it (verses 10,11). Any likeness to other of John's writings merely marks it as being Johannine in style.

It is sad to behold the way some Christians view the Second Epistles of Scripture. They seem to feel that Paul or Peter or John wrote an Epistle, and then sometime after concluding that Epistle, the writer discovered he had something more to say. And so he sat down to write a sort of appendage or addition to supplement those thoughts he omitted from the First Epistle. Now I never could bring myself to believe that the Holy Ghost forgot to put anything in any one book in the Bible. Such a thought is disparaging and derogatory to the full inspiration of the Holy Scriptures.

> *The elder unto the elect lady and her children,*
> *whom I love in the truth; and not I only, but also all*
> *they that have known the truth.*   2 JOHN 1

"The elder." John the elder is not a different person from John the Apostle. Peter, in his First Epistle, called himself both an "apostle" (1:1) and an "elder" (5:1). The word "elder" appears frequently in the Old Testament and it referred to the heads or leaders of the tribes and families. There were seventy who assisted Moses in matters of jurisprudence (Numbers 11:16; Deuteronomy 27:1). These elders were seniors, men advanced in life who looked after public affairs (Luke 7:3). In the Christian Church the elders were men of maturity in spiritual experience appointed to exercise spiritual oversight and care over the local assemblies. It seems quite clear that there was a plurality of elders in each local assembly (Acts 14:23; 20:17). The Greek word is *presbuteros,* and the elder's divine qualification is made clear in the Scriptures (1 Timothy 5:17; Titus 1:5-6). Inasmuch as the Greek word also means advanced in years or aged, it is possible that John used it in that sense. It is so used in Acts 2:17. John the Presbyter is the same person as John the Apostle.

"Unto the elect lady and her children." The Greek word for *lady* is *kyria,* and is the equivalent of the Hebrew "Martha." She was a Christian woman of some prominence in the Church and one who was likely esteemed by many. I do not take it that the "lady" here is the whole Church, but rather an individual woman who lived somewhere within bounds of the circuit of assemblies over which the Apostle John had oversight. This Second Epistle of John is the only book in the Bible addressed to a woman. In his salutation John included "her children." The lady herself

was one of God's elect, one of His called-out ones, a member of His true Church.

"Whom I love in the truth." The aged apostle writes that he loves this lady and her children. The word for *love* here is *agapaō,* not *phileō.* He uses the word for divine love, not mere human fondness. It would have been a serious mistake for him to use the latter term. With all sincerity, respect, and purity he loved this family with true Christian love, a love circumscribed by the truth as it is in Christ Jesus our Lord.

> *. . . and not I only, but also all they that have known the truth; For the truth's sake, which dwelleth in us, and shall be with us for ever.*   2 JOHN 1-2

The love with which John loved this woman and her children was bound by the truth; that is, I take it, he and others loved her because her Christian life exemplified the truth as it is in the Word of God. You can see from this what the love of the truth will do; it binds together all who know experientially the truth. A popular theology of our present day teaches that we are to love one another and never mind differences of opinion. We are told that we must put up with the divergence of theological thought and concentrate on loving one another. I have no quarrel with the man who tells me I am to love my neighbor, but let me make myself clear on the point that truth must never be surrendered. The apostle is speaking here of *"love in the truth . . . for the truth's sake"* among them that are *"walking in truth."* Not far from our branch church in Southfield there stands a community church. One of its members invited one of our members to visit there. He said, "Our church is the kind where Jews, Roman Catholics, and Protestants worship together and no one is ever offended." I can tell you now that no true believer in the Lord Jesus Christ can remain in that church without surrendering the truth. John emphasizes faithfulness to the truth. Paul withdrew himself from them that "walked not uprightly according to the truth of the gospel" (Galatians 2:11-14). And so must we! It is the truth of God that binds hearts together because the truth is the basis of all divine righteousness, thus "we can do nothing against the truth, but for the truth" (2 Corinthians 13:8).

> *Grace be with you, mercy, and peace, from God the Father, and from the Lord Jesus Christ, the Son of the Father, in truth and love.* 2 JOHN 3

In his salutation John invokes the threefold blessing of *grace, mercy, and peace.* An interesting observation at this point is that this threefold invocation of grace, mercy, and peace, when it appears in the salutation in any of the Epistles, is addressed to individuals (1 Timothy 1:2; 2 Timothy 1:2; Titus 1:4; 2 John 3). This lends added weight in favor of the argument that John wrote his Second Epistle to an individual and not to the Church. It is the individual who needs mercy. This word *mercy* (Greek, *eleos*) assumes need on the part of him who receives it. Mercy is that act of God whereby He outwardly manifests pity and sympathy toward an individual. And you might have noticed that wherever the words "mercy" and "peace" are found together, they appear in that order, except in Galatians 6:16. Peace is the resulting experience in the heart of the man who has been the recipient of God's mercy. And who among us does not need God's compassion and mercy daily? "It is of the LORD's mercies that we are not consumed, because His compassions fail not. They are new every morning: great is Thy faithfulness" (Lamentations 3:22-23).

Grace, mercy, and peace come from *"God the Father,*

and from the Lord Jesus Christ, the Son of the Father" (verse 3). An important observation in this statement is that God is the source of grace, mercy, and peace. But more important than this, I believe, is the perfect equality between the Father and the Son. Both the Father and the Son are the immediate personal source, because both are coequal and coeternal. Any denial of the Son is a denial of the Father, and all such denials characterize antichrist (1 John 2:22-23; 4:2-3). Christianity is Christ, thus any attempt to disassociate the Son from the Father is a denial of the basic and essential fact of the historic Biblical position. Apart from the only begotten Son no man can know the Father (John 1:18; 14:6-11). On another occasion Jesus said, "And he that seeth Me seeth Him that sent Me" (John 12:45). I believe that this is the idea in verse 9 of this Second Epistle of John: *"Whosoever transgresseth, and abideth not in the doctrine of Christ, hath not God. He that abideth in the doctrine of Christ, he hath both the Father and the Son."*

I rejoiced greatly that I found of thy children walking in truth, as we have received a commandment from the Father. 2 JOHN 4

In an age marked by perilous times, which times are characterized, among other things, by disobedience to parents (2 Timothy 3:2), it is refreshing to hear of one's children living for God. John's heart was made to rejoice in this. Here was a Christian home in the midst of paganism and ungodliness. Of his own spiritual children, John wrote later, "I have no greater joy than to hear that my children walk in truth" (3 John 4). We are sometimes disappointed in the kind of lives some young people in our churches are living, but it is most refreshing indeed to meet those whose words and deeds are circumscribed by the Word of God.

Very often our behavior reflects upon our home training [or lack of it], or upon our obedience or disobedience to the instructions we received from our parents.

And now I beseech thee, lady, not as though I wrote a new commandment unto thee, but that which we had from the beginning, that we love one another.

2 JOHN 5

The apostle speaks further of love when he exhorts, *"And now I beseech thee, lady, not as though I wrote a new commandment unto thee, but that which we had from the beginning, that we love one another."* Here John is rehearsing a similar thought found frequently in his writings. Not less than thirteen times in the New Testament Christ's followers are exhorted to "love one another." Of this number, ten appearances are from the pen of John the Apostle. Certainly we cannot place too much emphasis upon a subject the Holy Spirit reiterates so frequently. And yet this greatest Christian characteristic is conspicuous by its absence. It seems as though we learn a little about almost everything in this life, but we are slow in learning how to get along with one another. It is not expected that we will all agree on all points, but we had better be careful on what points and in what spirit we disagree. The commandment to "love one another" has been enjoined upon the Christian Church since its beginning, and it is likewise enjoined upon each individual Christian from the beginning of his Christian experience. The love with which one saint is to love another saint is that divine love which, in its very essence, is self-sacrificial as displayed by God in Christ's death at Calvary (John 3:16; Romans 5:8). Kenneth S. Wuest points out that the words "one another" are a reciprocal pronoun in the Greek text. That is, there must be reciprocity among the saints as to this love. A saint must reciprocate the love shown him by a fellow saint.

The Apostle Paul wrote, "This love of which I speak is slow to lose patience—it looks for a way of being constructive. It is not possessive: it is neither anxious to impress nor does it cherish inflated ideas of its own importance. Love has good manners and does not pursue selfish advantage. It is not touchy. It does not keep account of evil or gloat over the wickedness of other people. On the contrary, it is glad with all good men when truth prevails. Love knows no limit to its endurance, no end to its trust, no fading of its hope: it can outlast anything. It is, in fact, the one thing that still stands when all else has fallen" (1 Corinthians 13:4-7, J. B. Phillips translation). My friend Dr. Vincent Brushwyler, told of an experience during one of his visits to Africa. A group of missionaries, working under the Conservative Baptist Foreign Missionary Society, were engaged in translation work among primitive tribes. Unable to find a word for *love* in the dialect of one of the tribes, the translators continued to question the members of that tribe. Their patient and prayerful interrogation eventually brought forth fruit when one of the tribe members responded with, "Oh, you mean to have his interest inside of me." This to me expresses adequately the meaning of the love of which John speaks.

And this is love, that we walk after His commandments. This is the commandment, That, as ye have heard from the beginning, ye should walk in it.

2 JOHN 6

But what is this love of which John writes? He describes it thus, *"And this is love, that we walk after His commandments. This is the commandment, That, as ye have heard from the beginning, ye should walk in it."* This is the second time in this Epistle the apostle uses the expression *"from the beginning."* Here in verse 6 he speaks of *"commandments"* and of *"the commandment."* The singular always refers to the one specific commandment to "love one another." The commandment appears five times in the First Epistle (3:11,23; 4:7,11,12). It was that which the disciples heard from our Lord "from the beginning" of His public ministry (John 13:34-35).

> *For many deceivers are entered into the world, who confess not that Jesus Christ is come in the flesh. This is a deceiver and an antichrist.*   2 JOHN 7

John now refers to a class of people who were known as Gnostics. This sect denied the humanity of our Lord, that is, they held Him to be merely an appearance, only a phantom, thereby denying the Incarnation, the fact that God actually was manifest in flesh. John faced this problem in the First Epistle (1 John 4:2-3), and now he expresses concern lest the woman and her children fall prey to such false teachers. The presence of these roving imposters who corrupt men's minds posed a deadly threat with their heresies. They were not in agreement with the doctrines of the Church when they denied that "the Word was made flesh" (John 1:14), that "God was in Christ, reconciling the world unto Himself" (2 Corinthians 5:19) and that "God was manifest in the flesh" (1 Timothy 3:16). The pattern of all false teachers and false teachings is to aim at the very foundation of the faith by attacking the Person of our Lord Jesus Christ. All such are deceivers and they must be exposed for what they are. Beware of these corrupters of men's minds (2 Corinthians 11:3).

> *Look to yourselves, that we lose not those things which we have wrought, but that we receive a full reward.*   2 JOHN 8

Here they are called upon to consider what losses would be suffered by permitting themselves to become sidetracked from the truth. When John says, *"Look to yourselves,"* he is not suggesting that the members of this family be self-dependent and thereby independent of God. He merely warns them that they must ever be watchful, keeping an eye upon themselves. I have felt at times that we Christians have been guilty of failing to exercise the proper care over ourselves. The Scriptures exhort us to examine ourselves (2 Corinthians 13:5), to build up ourselves in our most holy faith (Jude 20), to keep ourselves in the love of God (Jude 21), to keep ourselves from idols (1 John 5:21). There is no thought in John's words of the Christian's losing the salvation which God has bestowed upon each believing sinner freely by His grace. The loss here has to do with rewards, not salvation. We are warned against forfeiting the reward of our labor. Paul wrote, "Let no man beguile you of your reward" (Colossians 2:18).

Whosoever transgresseth, and abideth not in the doctrine of Christ, hath not God. He that abideth in the doctrine of Christ, he hath both the Father and the Son.   2 JOHN 9

Twice in this one verse we read the phrase *"the doctrine of Christ."* The word *doctrine* (Greek, *didache*) means "teaching." John is not referring here merely to those doctrines which Christ taught, but rather teaching with reference to Christ, teaching which recognizes Jesus as the Messiah and Saviour. The word *transgresseth* (Greek, *parabaino*) means "to go beyond." Here we have the key to the understanding of the sin with which John is dealing. In John's day, as in our own, there were those men who boasted their intellectual progress and went beyond the revelation of God. Almost all of the better known modern cults profess to have some new thought which the rest of us have missed. But God condemns the proud claims of all who go beyond that which He has written. Let the "advanced thinkers" and "intellectuals" of our day take heed lest, in their boasted progress, they drift away from Christ instead of progressing toward Him. One mark of the true believer in Christ is the fact that he clings to Christ and to the Word of God. Let us not be sidetracked by modern intellectualism and the new thought of our day which goes beyond what God has written.

> *If there come any unto you, and bring not this doctrine, receive him not into your house, neither bid him God speed: For he that biddeth him God speed is partaker of his evil deeds.*   2 JOHN 10-11

In view here are the false teachers who come with false teachings. They do not believe nor teach the true doctrine, namely, that Christ is God manifest in flesh. These teachers are not Christians at all. They are not true witnesses of Jehovah; they are actually the devil's witnesses. Satan is quite clever. When he comes he does so "transformed into an angel of light" (2 Corinthians 11:14-15). He brainwashes his victims so that falsehood appears to them as truth. Through his subtle wiles he deceived Eve and dragged the whole human race into sin (Genesis 3:1-7). Now there are many such teachers in the world today, some of whom are quite zealous to spread their pernicious doctrine. Christians are not to welcome them nor bid them Godspeed in their departure. We are forbidden to show hospitality to the enemies of the faith, for in so doing we become partners with them in the disseminating of heresy. The apostle is not condoning any act of impoliteness on the part of the Christian, but he does condemn any fraternizing with any and all who oppose the truth. Early in the

Church's history local assemblies met in homes (Romans 16:5; Colossians 4:15), therefore those traveling teachers needed watching lest they creep in unawares.

Having many things to write unto you, I would not write with paper and ink: but I trust to come unto you, and speak face to face, that our joy may be full.
2 JOHN 12

John had written all that the Holy Spirit told him to write. Here is sufficient warning against the heretics. In his heart there were some more thoughts he would have liked to convey to "the elect lady and her children" on these very matters. These things John felt would contribute to their maintaining their present state of the fullness of joy; however, they must wait until such time as they can speak face to face.

The children of thy elect sister greet thee. Amen.
2 JOHN 13

John concludes this brief, personal letter by conveying greetings. We do not know who the "elect sister" is, hence we have no way of knowing who her children are. It really does not matter, so it is foolish to speculate. God knows her name and the names of her children. We know she was a Christian. So be it! This personal note adds to an already lovely little letter. Amen.

THE THIRD EPISTLE
OF
JOHN

XXI. THE THIRD EPISTLE OF JOHN

The writer of this Epistle styles himself the Elder [or Presbyter] as he did in his Second Epistle. As in the Second, John addresses himself to an individual. This is a divinely-inspired personal letter. It was written to a man named Gaius. A Gaius is mentioned at least four times more in the New Testament (Acts 19:29; 20:4; Romans 16:23; 1 Corinthians 1:14), but it is uncertain as to whether the Gaius to whom John writes here is the same person who figured in Paul's life and labors.

The names of three men are mentioned in the Epistle, and it is concerning these that the Holy Spirit addresses

Himself through the pen of John. Gaius is spoken of first, for it is to him the Epistle is written.

A.   *Gaius the Practicing Christian* (verses 1-8).

   1. *The Designation of Gaius* (verse 1).

   The elder unto the well-beloved Gaius, whom I love in the truth.   3 JOHN 1

Gaius is called "beloved" four times in this brief Epistle (verses 1,2,5,11). The word is used here as an adjective describing this man as highly regarded among brethren because he was in good stead with God. This form of address is used only among believers, "the elect of God, holy and *beloved*" (Colossians 3:12). While God loves all men unconditionally (John 3:16), He loves His own children in a special sense. On numerous occasions He referred to Christ as "My *beloved* Son" (Matthew 3:17; 12:18; 17:5). Thus to all who love the Lord Jesus Christ, the Father extends that same measure of love. When Christ spoke to the Father concerning those who loved Him, He said, "That the world may know that Thou hast . . . loved them, as Thou hast loved Me" (John 17:23). Earlier in one of His famous discourses He said, "He that loveth Me shall be loved of My Father" (John 14:21) and "If a man love Me . . . My Father will love him" (John 14:23), and again, "For the Father Himself loveth you, because ye have loved Me" (John 16:27). Since we are "accepted in the beloved [Christ]" (Ephesians 1:6), we too are God's *beloved* ones. Peter, Paul, and John used this term frequently in their writings. It is the Holy Spirit's designation of the children of God. (See 2 Peter 3:1,8,14,15,17 and 1 John 3:2,21; 4:1,7,11.) Gaius was a beloved one in Christ.

2. *The Desire for Gaius* (verse 2).

*Beloved, I wish above all things that thou mayest
prosper and be in health, even as thy soul prospereth.*

3 JOHN 2

The spiritual health of Gaius was robust. In his inner
heart-life Gaius had been traveling a good road. Life for
him had been a spiritually prosperous journey up to the
time John had written to him, and there is nothing in
Scripture to indicate that Gaius ever departed from the
straight and narrow way. The Church of Christ needs more
like him for she is plagued with sick saints. Many Christians are diet-conscious as regards the body but they give
little or no attention to the soul. Today we see so much
which is the very opposite from Gaius' condition. There
is more bodily vigor than spiritual health. We may deduce
from this verse that sound physical health does not always
accompany sound spiritual health. The Church is beset
with many and varied dangers from without, but none are
so damaging right now as the spiritually sick saints within.
God help us!

3. *The Delight in Gaius* (verses 3-4).

*For I rejoiced greatly, when the brethren came and
testified of the truth that is in thee, even as thou walk-
est in the truth.*

3 JOHN 3

The Christian teachers who had gone out from Ephesus
to spread the Word of God had frequently brought the
apostles word concerning other believers. At times the news
was not good, but with reference to Gaius the news de-
lighted the apostle's heart. Whenever traveling preachers
came through they had a good word for the beloved Gaius.
The word *came* in the Greek text is a present participle and

denotes continuous action. The brethren kept coming with testimonies to the genuine Christian experience of this man of God. What was the secret of his soul prosperity? The *truth* was in him and he walked in the *truth*. Gaius was a man of God's Word. He read and studied the Scriptures and then put what he learned into practice. I have met some Christians who make a boast of knowing the truth but who fail to manifest the truth in words and deeds. For these I could pray earnestly that they might prosper spiritually to the extent that they have prospered physically and materially. But in the case of Gaius the *truth* was dwelling richly in a frail body (Colossians 3:16), thus he could say, "It is well with my soul." When some saints sit in church and sing, "It is well with my soul," they are merely whistling in the dark, deceiving themselves. Gaius' life expressed the truth he loved. He adorned the doctrine he believed. Gaius and the truth had an inherent relationship.

> *I have no greater joy than to hear that my children walk in truth.*   3 JOHN 4

Was Gaius one of John's converts or was he merely a member of an assembly under John's care? The use of the word "my" would seem to indicate that Gaius was a convert of John, and the apostle says that his heart reaches its highest point of joy when he sees those whom he has led to Christ living consistently and sincerely for Christ's glory. Paul expressed somewhat the same idea when he called his converts at Philippi "my joy and crown" (Philippians 4:1), and then exhorted them to "stand fast in the Lord." (See also 1 Thessalonians 2:19-20.) It is a heart-breaking experience for pastors, evangelists, and missionaries to see those who have made a profession of faith in Christ fall by the way. Any man who has sufficient compassion to pray for the lost and witness to them will most certainly be jealous for the spiritual growth of those whom he leads to make a profession of faith in Christ. Paul wrote to the Corinthians, "I write not these things to shame you, but as my beloved sons I warn you" (1 Corinthians 4:14). There was sternness in the apostle's dealings with the Corinthians but there was tenderness also. His purpose was not to embarrass them, but as a loving father would rebuke his own children in the spirit of love, so Paul would lead his converts into a closer fellowship with the Lord. He was jealous over them with godly jealousy (2 Corinthians 11:2). We have no greater joy than to hear that our children walk in truth.

4. *The Diligence of Gaius* (verses 5-7).

Beloved, thou doest faithfully whatsoever thou doest to the brethren, and to strangers.   3 JOHN 5

The apostle commends Gaius for the hospitality he showed toward traveling preachers and teachers. Gaius performed this service as a regular practice, extending it even to those with whom he was not acquainted. What an encouragement Gaius must have been to those servants of Jesus Christ! Entertaining Christians in early times was of peculiar importance because they were poor and persecuted and would need the offered help (Matthew 10:23; Acts 8:1). Had Gaius been a member of some tight assembly of the saints, where barriers are raised up to keep out the stranger, he would have lost both the blessing of serving and the reward. Moreover this word of commendation could not have been written of him. Gaius was "distributing to the necessity of saints; given to hospitality" (Romans 12:13), a requirement for an oversight man in the assembly (1 Timothy 3:2; Titus 1:8). And who knows whether or not he entertained angels unawares (Hebrews 13:2)? It was so in the cases of Abraham (Genesis 18:1-3) and Lot (Genesis 19:1-3). "For God is not unrighteous to forget your work and labour of love, which ye have shewed toward His name, in that ye have ministered to the saints, and do minister" (Hebrews 6:10). Gaius met the major requirement for stewardship; he was faithful (1 Corinthians 4:2).

> *Which have borne witness of thy charity before the church: whom if thou bring forward on their journey after a godly sort, thou shalt do well: Because that for His name's sake they went forth, taking nothing of the Gentiles.* 3 JOHN 6-7

The two occurrences of the word "doest" in verse 5 emphasize the fact that Gaius repeatedly and continuously engaged in caring for the needs of the Lord's servants. These testified that it was a loving service. The word *charity* (Greek, *agapē*) should be translated "love" since it is the particular word used for divine love. This is the love that God is in His very nature (1 John 4:8,16), and it is the love which is shed abroad in our hearts by the Holy Spirit. (Compare Romans 5:5 with 2 Peter 1:4.) It leads the list of the ninefold fruit of the spirit (Galatians 5:22). Whenever these traveling ministers passed through Ephesus and visited the assembly of the saints, they testified to the loving hospitality of Gaius. He always welcomed the traveler into his home and then sent him on his way in a manner worthy of God, and in so doing he did well (1 John 3:17-18). Gaius realized that the Lord's work should be supported by the Lord's people. This is the correct pattern of a true Christian ministry. The servant of the Lord must go forth depending only upon the Lord. He must preach the gospel of Christ without charge (1 Corinthians 9:18; 1 Thessalonians 2:9). But all of God's people should manifest the loving hospitality of Gaius so that the servants of Christ need not look to the world for support. John says that "we ought" [or *owe it*] to become fellow helpers with those who preach and teach the truth. Such was Gaius, the practicing Christian.

B. *Diotrephes the Proud Christian* (verses 9-11).

1. *His Personal Ambition* (verse 9).

I wrote unto the church: but Diotrephes, who loveth to have the preeminence among them, receiveth us not.

3 JOHN 9

John had evidently written earlier to this assembly. This could have been his First Epistle, or some other letter not known to us today. However, this is not important. What is important is the lesson we all need to learn from the life of Diotrephes. He was a man with a personal ambition. John writes, "He loveth to have the preeminence." The word *preeminence* comes from two Greek words which mean, "to be fond of being first." Diotrephes was a little pope. He was actually trampling underfoot the truth of the headship of Christ over the Church. There are only two places in the New Testament where the word "preeminence" appears, here in 3 John 9 and in Colossians 1:18 where we read, "And He is the head of the body, the church: who is the beginning, the firstborn from the dead; that in all things He might have the *preeminence*." Diotrephes thought more highly of himself than he did of Christ. He could not say with John the Baptist, "He must increase, but I must decrease" (John 3:30). Someone has said, "Diotrephes is the father of a long line of sons who have not learned to distinguish between love for Christ and His Church and love for their own place in it." It is told of Dr. Lee Robertson that he wrote an article on Diotrephes for a denominational paper, and the editor told him that twenty-five officials in the church stopped the paper to show their resentment against being personally attacked. These are the offspring of Diotrephes who reject the authority of Christ and take it to themselves.

2. *His Perverted Actions* (verse 9).

John wrote that he *"receiveth us not."* In contrast to the actions of Gaius, he refused to receive even the Apostle John himself. He showed no hospitality toward John and refused to recognize John's authority as an apostle. Possibly he felt that by refusing to accept John he might gain more prestige for himself. The self-centered Christian who loves to have the preeminence cannot stand the brother who towers above him in spiritual stature. He believes that through holding others down he can rise above them. Here is a man who so loved power that he was ready to cause others to suffer in order to attain it. He was concerned only about his own position and importance. Such action is a perversion of proper Christian behavior.

> *Wherefore, if I come, I will remember his deeds which he doeth, prating against us with malicious words. . . .* 3 JOHN 10

John describes the actions of Diotrephes further in the words, *"prating against us."* The word *prate* signifies to talk as a babbler, to raise false accusations. In 1 Timothy 5:13 it is rendered "tattlers." These go about "speaking things which they ought not." Here is an unholy practice which is too prevalent among Christians. The human tongue is a little member, but I fear we underestimate the possible extent of its destructive powers (James 3:3-8).

There are some things we *ought* [or owe it] to do. We "*ought* always to pray, and not to faint" (Luke 18:1). "We *ought* to obey God rather than men" (Acts 5:29). We "*ought* to bear the infirmities of the weak" (Romans 15:1). "We *ought* also to love one another" (1 John 4:11). We *ought* to be hospitable toward fellow believers (3 John 8). But there is one thing we ought [or owe it] *not* to do, and that is to speak wrongly, or unnecessarily of others (1 Timothy 5:13; Titus 1:11). "My brethren, these things *ought not* so to be" (James 3:10). In his ambition to be preeminent, Diotrephes could not do what he ought to have done, and that is to pray, "Set a watch, O Lord, before my mouth; keep the door of my lips" (Psalm 141:3). Instead, he spoke "malicious" [wicked, vicious] words against the servants of Jesus Christ, thereby doing that which he ought not to have done. I say again that his actions were a perversion of proper Christian behavior.

> . . . *Neither doth he himself receive the brethren, and forbiddeth them that would, and casteth them out of the church.*   3 JOHN 10

Diotrephes not only refused to accept the itinerant teachers but he sought to prevent other brethren from so doing. And, as though such actions were not bad enough, he literally excommunicated them who would not comply with his demands. This is a terrible evil which exists in some assemblies even today. It was to the oversight brethren in the assembly that Peter wrote, "Neither as being lords over God's heritage, but being ensamples to the flock" (1 Peter 5:3). Domineering men who lord it over God's flock do injury to His holy cause. Jesus said, "Ye know that the princes of the Gentiles exercise dominion over them, and they that are great exercise authority upon them. But it shall not be so among you: but whosoever will be great among you, let him be your minister" (Matthew 20:25-26). The Bible warns against both love of money (1 Peter 5:2; 1 Timothy 6:10) and love of power. Now such warning does not do away with the divinely-ordered, scripturally-exercised authority in the local assembly. This is encouraged in 1 Thessalonians 5:12; 1 Timothy 5:17; and Hebrews 13:7. There must be rule in the assembly, and there cannot be rule without rulers, but there is no place for the Diotrephes type.

3. *Some Practical Advice* (verse 11).

Beloved, follow not that which is evil, but that which is good. He that doeth good is of God: but he that doeth evil hath not seen God.　　　3 JOHN 11

In the minds of some Bible teachers this verse contains the strong implication that Diotrephes may not have been a true Christian at all, but a mere professor only. How, then, did he get into the local assembly and rise to power? The answer is not hard to find if we will but look within ourselves. In most churches there has been a lowering of the standards to the extent of compromise. Diotrephes is not carefully screened by spiritual, Bible-taught men of God. We extend to him the "right hand of fellowship." For a while he wins friends and influences people, and then one day he shows his real self.

The solemn advice here is that such a man is not to be followed; he is not to be imitated or mimicked. Too often Diotrephes becomes a hero in the minds of some because he seems to be championing a cause. But the only cause he defends is his own. And if Gaius is of a meek and quiet spirit, and it seems that he might have been, then he might just go along quietly with Diotrephes in order to keep the peace. However, the apostle exhorts him not to do it. The difference between right and wrong is irreconcilable. Even though Diotrephes might be a man of wealth and influence, he is an evil man because he insists that he must increase and Christ must decrease.

The exhortation is one with which every Christian should be occupied, namely, *"Follow not that which is evil, but that which is good."* The word *follow* means to imitate, to mimic. We are all imitators from earliest childhood. Children are fond of playing follow-the-leader. Now, it is bad enough when the unsaved and unchurched set a poor example for others, but when the Christian and those in the local assembly engage in sinful and questionable practices, it is sadder still. How frequently we fail to realize that by our words and actions we lead others! John's word here is a warning to all believers not to follow the Diotrephes type. We are to follow after love (1 Corinthians 14:1), that which is good (1 Thessalonians 5:15), righteousness (1 Timothy 6:11; 2 Timothy 2:22), peace (Hebrews 12:14) and in the steps of our Lord (1 Peter 2:21), but never let us mimic or imitate a Diotrephes. Let us follow on to know the Lord (Hosea 6:3) and not afar off as did Peter (Luke 22:54).

C. *Demetrius the Praiseworthy Christian* (verses 12-14).

We come now to the last of the three men mentioned in this Epistle. It would seem from verse 12 that Gaius did not know Demetrius. He might have been one of those whom Diotrephes refused to receive. Some teachers believe that Demetrius was the bearer of this letter to Gaius.

1. *The Testimony Concerning Demetrius* (verse 12).

Demetrius hath good report of all men, and of the truth itself: yea, and we also bear record: and ye know that our record is true.   3 JOHN 12

The testimony of this man's Christian character stood up with consistency. Non-Christians were impressed by his life. It is an essential requirement for Christian service that we be "men of honest report" (Acts 6:3), that is, men of good reputation such as were Cornelius (Acts 10:22), Timothy (Acts 16:2), Ananias (Acts 22:12), and others. These men were bearing a good witness for Christ and that witness was making its mark in the lives of others.

2. *The Truth Controlling Demetrius* (verse 12).

The Christian of "good report" is the man who keeps God's Word. The "truth" itself testified in behalf of Demetrius. His life harmonized with the teachings of Christ and the apostles. To all of this evidence John adds his own testimony, *"and we also bear record: and ye know that our record is true"* (verse 12). How wonderful when the life of any child of God can have so complete a witness!

I had many things to write, but I will not with ink and pen write unto thee: But I trust I shall shortly see thee, and we shall speak face to face. Peace be to thee. Our friends salute thee. Greet the friends by name.   3 JOHN 13-14

John closes this Epistle on a note similar to that in the Second Epistle. He could think of many things he would like to write but they must await his meeting Gaius face to face (verse 13). He wishes peace for Gaius, sends greetings from mutual friends, and requests Gaius to convey his own personal greetings to his friends. In a longer letter, such as Paul's Epistle to the Colossians, he might have named each one and said something appropriate for each. But that must wait until some later date, possibly when they [and we] are gathered together to meet the Lord in the air. What a greeting day that will be!

BIBLIOGRAPHY

CALVIN, JOHN. *The Catholic Epistles*. Grand Rapids, Michigan: Eerdmans.

CANDLISH, ROBERT S. *The First Epistle of John*. Grand Rapids, Michigan: Zondervan.

Clark's Theology Library, Volume 8. Edinburgh: T. and T. Clark.

DARBY, J. N. *Nine Lectures on The First Epistle of John*. Oak Park, Illinois: Bible Truth Publishers.

EBRARD, JOHN H. A. *The Epistles of St. John*. Edinburgh: T. and T. Clark.

ELLICOTT, CHARLES JOHN. ed. *The Epistles of Peter, John and Jude*. Grand Rapids, Michigan: Zondervan.

ERDMAN, CHARLES R. *The General Epistles*. Philadelphia: The Westminster Press.

GOODMAN, GEORGE. *The Epistle of Eternal Life*. London: Pickering and Inglis.

HAUPT, ERICH. *The First Epistle of St. John*. Edinburgh: T. and T. Clark.

IRONSIDE, H. A. *Addresses on the Epistles of John*. New York: Loizeaux Brothers.

KING, GUY H. *The Fellowship*. London: Marshall, Morgan and Scott Ltd.

LAURIN, ROY L. *Life at Its Best*. Chicago, Illinois: Van Kampen Press.

LINCOLN, WILLIAM. *The Epistles of John*. London: Pickering and Inglis

LIAS, J. J. *The First Epistle of St. John*. London: Nisbet and Co.

LOVELESS, WENDELL P. *Studies In the Epistles of John*. Unpublished.

MORGAN, JAMES. *An Exposition of the First Epistle of John*. Edinburgh: T. and T. Clark.

The Pulpit Commentary. London: Randolph and Co.

Ross, Alexander. *Epistles of James and John* (New International Commentary on the New Testament). Grand Rapids, Michigan: Eerdmans.

Sadler, M. F. *The Epistles of Peter, James, John, and Jude.* London: George Bell and Sons.

Simpson, A. B. *The Epistles of Peter, John and Jude.* Harrisburg, Pennsylvania: Christian Publications Inc.

Smith, H. Framer. *Partnership with Deity.* Published by the author.

Strauss, Lehman. *Herein Is Love.* Published by the author.

Thomas, W. H. Griffith. *The Apostle John.* London: Pickering and Inglis.

Tidwell, Josiah Blake. *John and His Five Books.* Grand Rapids, Michigan: Eerdmans.

Van Ryn, August. *The Epistles of John.* New York: Loizeaux Brothers.

Vine, W. E. *The First Epistle of St. John.* London: Pickering and Inglis.

Westcott, Brooke Foss. *The Epistles of St. John.* Grand Rapids, Michigan: Eerdmans.

Wuest, Kenneth S. *In These Last Days.* Grand Rapids, Michigan: Eerdmans.

INDEX OF SCRIPTURE TEXTS

175

INDEX